FULL DISCLOSURE

Dagan J. Sharpe

Dagan J. Sharpe

ISBN: 0692985786
ISBN-13: 978-0692985786

DEDICATION

This book is dedicated to my loving wife, who has supported me through thick and thin. Even when I was blinded by selfish ambition, she saw through to my heart, and the potential man I could become in Christ. She never gave up hope, gave up faith, or gave up praying – and still doesn't.

Dagan J. Sharpe

CONTENTS

Dagan J. Sharpe

INTRODUCTION

Wake-Up Call

"A time comes when you need to stop waiting for the man you want to become & start being the man you want to be".[1]

- Bruce Springsteen

I wrote my first book shortly after the most pivotal moment in my life. Although getting married and witnessing the births of my children are clearly some of my most impactful moments, it's the time I almost lost everything that tops them all.

The blunt truth is I had my perspective and order of priorities all mixed up. I have always been a driven and competitive person, but I had lost sight of what was most important. Quite simply, the pursuit for more, was costing me more than I could have ever imagined, and I have a strong hunch, I'm not the only one blinded by this ancient, yet powerful lie - that our self-worth is tied to our net worth. I had heard this expression used over the years, but it never truly sunk in, until the moment I realized I had bought into the lie.

7

Throughout my financial career, I have found many people view wealth and riches as having an abundant supply of money. However, the actual definition of wealth is having an abundant supply of a *desirable* thing.[2] Clearly, all we most desire isn't limited to just money, but we can easily get caught up living like it is. This is what happened to me.

I desired a loving and close family. I desired good health, and I desired financial independence, but I was sacrificing everything for only one of those goals. For I had let myself get completely out of shape, and I was blindly short-changing my family of time together. As a result, my marriage wasn't what I knew it could be and my relationship with my children wasn't all it needed to be. It was after this realization that cumulated from a health scare and a night of significant disagreement with my wife that I saw the horror of what my life was becoming.

I was living for money and all these precious gifts I had been given were being squandered - my wife, my kids, and my health. This realization brought me to my knees and took me to my Heavenly Father, whom I hadn't spoken to in quite a while. In fact, He had been the most neglected of all.

I believed in Jesus Christ as my Savior, but never did much past that. He definitely wasn't a part of my life, consideration, or motivation. He wasn't my Lord, but that dramatic night, all that changed. I cried out to Him. I admitted to blowing it. I apologized for being so selfish and pleaded for His help. The good news is He came to my rescue. Over time, He literally took me from a condition of bedlam to bedrock.

That's what motivated me to write my first book, but I wanted to write it to a secular audience, caught up in wanting monetary riches. I wanted to write a book they would pick up. One they would read. For I rarely read Christian books, or was motivated to do so back then. All my books were business and financial books - not a bad thing, but this is the same audience I wanted to try and reach out to.

Now, as years have passed, and my walk with God has grown, I want to be out front with this simple truth - this is a Christian book, written from a Biblical world view and perspective. For in the end, in Christ is the only place true riches are found.

Money has its place, and the Bible speaks a lot about money, but that's not all there is to it. We are to be good stewards of all the resources God has given us and this includes finances, family, fitness (our health), and our faith. But it's only when we put Him first that these other areas can be properly managed.

I hope this doesn't turn some of you off and make you decide to put this book down. Please don't. For to be truly successful and rich in life, we must think beyond money, possessions, pleasures, positions and power. We must shift our primary pursuits and get them in proper perspective so that we can be most effective with the time we have left.

Actions create results, and far too many of us only dream about what we want, or unknowingly place limits on ourselves. We do this by failing to create plans, writing them down and then doing what is required to make our dreams reality.

This is true for all our goals and desires. Ever wonder how some folks seem to get so much accomplished and done? Quite often it is because they are intentional about getting things done and they are passionate and focused on doing it. Likewise, when it comes to our faith, families, fitness, and finances, we must make a plan, prioritize them and take action.

10

As the saying goes, "going a yard is hard, but an inch is a synch".[3] So, are you willing to take baby steps to make your dreams a reality? If so, this makes you part of the minority, rather than the majority.

Full Disclosure is a book filled with candid confessions from a "recovering workaholic" and offers insights to help others prone to this same condition.

One of these empowering benefits is the development of what I call our financial IQ. Being responsible and wise money managers is a requirement of good stewardship. The good news is if I can learn it, anyone can. For there was a time I couldn't even balance my own checkbook.

Today, my financial background includes serving as a licensed wealth consultant at a top international financial firm, and leading state, regional, and national initiatives for a Fortune 500 financial institution encompassing commercial banking, consumer, private banking, and trust.

I hold various investment and insurance licenses, as well as a real estate license.

However, I have learned from my clients and mentors who taught me more financial knowledge and savvy than I could have ever gained on my own. Building our financial IQs is important, and I look forward to sharing this information with you.

I'll also share lessons learned from mistakes made – which have been plenty. I am forever grateful for these lessons and even though painful, I appreciate the hard times. For they reveal treasures that can help us lead more fruitful lives. Again, these insights are shared in this book and include not just the ones I've experienced, but the ones passed down to me.

Interestingly, many of the people I have met with millions in the bank can also be some of the most unhappy and unsettled. There are also individuals that make millions every year, but have nothing to show for it, because they spend every dime. Many have broken families, broken bodies, and broken hearts.

So, I ask you, does having or making millions make someone rich if they live in lonely homes, have detached children, neglected health and live in a depressed state? If that's wealthy, I don't want it.

My vision of wealth is very different today. It's no longer limited to money. Instead, I desire peace. A life filled with God and doing work that allows me to use whatever skills and gifts He has given me to help others so that as the Bible says, "they may see my good deeds, and glorify my God in heaven" (Matthew 5:16).

I desire a life filled with love flowing to and from my friends and family. To have a healthy mind and body full of clarity, energy, and vitality. To live without fear, because my faith is strong and my relationship with God is ablaze. To live a life of service, optimism, hope, and joy. To not worry and fret about money, but to rather understand its place and purpose. This is the ultimate wealth.

I once heard a story about a man who was friends with an NFL offensive lineman. This gentleman was invited to the gym to observe a training session and witnessed these giants lifting 400 and 450 pound weights. He saw them strain in pain to force each repetition, to create new muscle and grow stronger. When he left the gym, he realized a simple truth in life. "To grow strong, we must lift something heavy". I love that insight - it's so true! To grow in life and to better ourselves, we must take on the heavy, or hard stuff. Growing isn't easy, but it's possible. We grow stronger with each repetition.

If we are Christians, our faith in Jesus Christ should be the primary foundation in our life. Without Him, we have nothing solid to build upon. For our faith redefines the way we approach, pursue, perceive, and steward the gifts He has given us. These gifts include our health, our finances, and our families. When we see these things as gifts our perspective of them changes. We no longer want to take them for granted, or neglect them. In addition, they no longer possess the power to consume us either. We strive to get better and maximize our effectiveness in them because we realize we are entrusted to do so by God.

If we truly believe this, we begin to take our roles as stewards seriously, and our walk with Christ impacts how we interact with everything, especially money.

Simply making money is not our mission. Our family is not our mission and neither is our body. These are all important and God desires us to take them seriously, but the gospel is our mission. For we are called to make disciples wherever we go. This means as Christians our privilege as disciple makers includes how we interact with money, others, ourselves, and our families.

Money can have a powerful impact and ministry when we realize everything is God's, and we simply obey Him on how we use it - this admittedly can often times be easier said than done.

However, the same is true for our families. When we follow His direction, our family can become powerful testimonies, and the same is true for our health.

How well we care for our bodies speaks volumes about how we view His gifts. For the human body and the gift of life is profound. Yet, so many of us neglect it and blindly take it for granted – as I once did.

In summary, this book will focus on the four key gifts we have been given to steward.

The first, our **faith**, is the bedrock and primary foundation of our life. The Bible tells us that we have been given a measure of faith, and that we are to grow in our knowledge of the Lord and mature as believers.

Therefore, our faith is a gift to be stewarded and strengthened. In doing so, we become better managers in practically everything else.

Remember, some of the monetarily richest people are sometimes the most restless and unhappy – because money can never fill and satisfy the void only Christ can fill.

Now, I'm not saying faith will fix all problems, but I am saying it helps us keep our life purpose in focus and to see our problems through a different perspective.

This leads us to the other gift we have been entrusted with - **family**. There are many who can share what failure here can mean to our emotional, physical, and financial health!

Family is a precious gift, we must focus on it and never take it for granted, but like me, there are many who never learned how to contribute to a fruitful family - and without the Word of God guiding the way, I would have never learned.

This is a topic I am deeply passionate about and can't wait to discuss further in our family chapter. For me, learning my role as *Pastor, Provider, Protector, Prayer*, and *Preparer* have been priceless!

The gift of **fitness (health)** is essential to engaging

life to the fullest. For without good health, we're limited. Obviously, there are uncontrollable factors and incidents that can occur, but we can always do our best to make sure we stay lean, healthy, and energetic.

Good health builds self-confidence, enhances our positive mood and gives us the drive to keep our other gifts fully supported. It's always nice to reap the fruits of our labor, and without good health we lack the ability to fully pursue all the opportunities that come our way.

I mention the gift of **finances** last because if we are growing in our faith, family, and fitness, and possess the slightest desire to effectively steward our finances, our chances for success are greatly improved. For we have the essentials going for us, and we most likely possess the proper perspective, discipline, faith, support, and motivation to handle the money part - not in the amount we have necessarily, but in our level of contentment and contribution with what we have.

We will begin by expanding our financial IQ by sharing practical insights and strategy around the basics, i.e.: deposits, loans and investments. Since these are things most of us have - we should be educated on them.

However, let me encourage you to skip sections of this chapter and come back to them if you find them to be too detailed in content. I want to provide some basic principles and application to help us become better stewards in this area, but I realize it may be a bit academic in places. So, feel free to skip ahead - you can always come back when ready.

I

FINANCES

"Money has never yet made anyone rich".[4]

- Seneca

We're going to get into some detailed nuts and bolts information here. I realize this may put many to sleep, but remember, you're building your financial IQ and that takes some homework.

So, what does success in our finances look like? To me, it's freedom - and financial freedom is really having freedom from worry. It's not measured by how much we have, but rather, can we get to a position of paying our bills in a timely fashion. Not overspending, but learning the value of establishing savings, such as emergency savings, and long term savings. Can we take the occasional vacation, but most importantly, escape from being a poor financial steward and the anxiety that creates.

God expects us to be good stewards of our financial resources, and I believe there are three primary components to help us make this happen -

establishing a *spending plan, a savings plan* and *a giving plan.*

Developing these financial habits isn't always easy, but they do help to strengthen our financial IQ. For we begin to place controls on money, rather than having it control us. In time, it can mean we no longer have to live month to month, or even day to day. In addition, we grow into our positions of being wise stewards of God's resources, and reach a new level of breakthrough.

The three primary ways to achieve this breakthrough with money however, doesn't begin with tactics. For in order to become effective money managers, we must first redefine our perspective of money, ensure the proper prioritization of money, and then we can begin effective preparations for money.

PERSPECTIVE

Redefining our perspective on money is essential, because it's not about accumulation. Rather, it's about stewardship. How do we effectively manage it so that we aren't consumed by it? Do we view money as the solution to our problems, the answer to our dreams, and/or make it the primary pursuit in our life?

I'm reminded of David and Goliath. The Bible tells us that David "ran quickly" to meet Goliath on the battle field. For those that remember, Goliath was a giant of a man who was a fierce warrior and had the entire nation of Israel scared stiff – including their King. This is because everyone was fixated on the size of their problem. They were looking at the giant. David however doesn't appear to show even the slightest bit of fear. How can this be? Because he was looking past the giant and to the size of his God.

He saw past the problem. He looked to his Lord, and he knew His Lord was even greater than this temporary problem – no matter the size.

Likewise, so often we look to money. We look at this giant issue, either as a problem, or a solution, when we should be looking to God. He is our Source. Money is simply a tool. When our perspective is on Him, money gets put back to its proper size.

So, before anyone can effectively strengthen their financial IQ, it's vital they have the correct perspective. Yet, this is often missed. For we like to jump right into the tactics and strategies, before we get our heart right.

David had his heart right and as a result, his tactics were effective.

When our heart is right towards God, we too can exercise more effective tactics.

I don't know where your heart is in regards to God and money, but I pray you are in a surrendered position. Meaning, you acknowledge your role as a steward of God's resources and you have already settled the issue as to Who your Lord is.

To further illustrate the power of perspective, my mother and father married young and we didn't have much. They later divorced and for a while we had even less. Money was tight and I recall being teased because my pants were too long. My mom would buy them that way so they would last longer as I grew. Having pants rolled up several times over didn't place me in the popular crowd. So, at an early age, a desire for money began to grow. For I concluded, if we had more money, I wouldn't be teased, because I could afford the cool clothes.

We still see this today as adults don't we? Many buy extremely expensive shoes and clothes. Maybe because they can, or maybe because they desire to impress others?

We can tend to have a herd mentality at times that creates a need in us to want to run with the bulls - the strong and the powerful. We want the cool clothes, the cool cars, the cool house, the cool vacation – you get the idea.

Clearly, if we can afford all this stuff without going into debt and obsessing over them – okay, but even then, we must ask ourselves what we are truly chasing and why.

My wife is not vain, or materialistic in any way, and she doesn't seek designer trends. However, it is uncanny how whenever she is in a store she naturally gravitates to the most expensive items. Obviously, the more expensive something is it is typically because of its quality.

There is absolutely nothing wrong with wanting quality things and having nice things – again, I'm talking about our perspectives.

Do we somehow believe being able to afford expensive items improves our self-worth? This is a masterful lie many believe, as I once did - that our self-worth is tied to our net worth.

If we believe this, we become consumed with money and all that it can bring, at the expense of other things, because we have convinced ourselves internally that somehow the more we have, the higher our value becomes.

But to whom? What if we lose our job by no fault of our own, or get in an accident that prevents us from working, or countless other things happen that cause us to lose money? Does our value as people suddenly diminish too?

I recall a time when a round of displacements took place at a large corporation I once worked. Many lost their jobs and this sudden loss literally sent a person to the hospital. Their identity was caught up in their position that was taken away, and the shockwaves of this event sent this person crashing.

How often do we see this? People who once had much, either spend it all, like it was going to last forever, or lose it all by unforeseen and unfortunate events. As a result, they too spiral into a deep depression, panic, distress, and collapse.

This is not to criticize these people, but the point goes back to perspective. If we believe money and positon is our identity and validity as human beings, we are in for some rude awakenings.

This is why I so appreciate the story Jesus told of the rich young ruler in Mark 10. This young man had it all. He had fame, fortune, good reputation, and was honored by many. I'm sure he was generous with his wealth too, and because of his philanthropy, generosity, good looks, charm, ability and skill, he was like many of our modern day celebrities.

Yet, when he inquired of Jesus as to what was left for him to do to inherit eternal life, the answer left him saddened and disheartened. For I'm sure he felt he was a shoe-in, but Jesus knew his heart's devotion.

He knew money held this man captive and to be freed from this captivity, Jesus told him he must give all he had to the poor and follow Him. What an invitation! Follow God, in the flesh! Learn from the Creator of the universe – what could be better treasure than that? But we don't necessarily see it like that do we? Neither did this young man, for we know the story. Money was this man's deeper treasure and he couldn't release it – not even for God.

I cherish this story because when I'm being completely honest with myself – I see me in that man. I said I was a Christian. I said I followed Jesus, but I followed money and promotion more. And it was costing me dearly. For my faith was malnourished. I was rarely in church, rarely read my Bible and I definitely wasn't living like a Christian. As a result, our bank account may have been increasing, but my health, faith, and family were suffering for it. I was choosing to believe the lie – that my self-worth was tied to my net worth, and I was blindly pursing this lie to my own detriment.

I know I'm not alone. Others believe this lie too, and the story of the rich young ruler so perfectly illustrates how long the lie has been around and effective.

Thankfully, we can break free from this lie and many other falsehoods that surround money. Money is not evil. It has no power, but people can be evil and use it for destructive purposes to themselves and others.

However, it can be used for good purposes too. It can be a tool God entrusts to His children to promote His plans, and to be used by those committed to building His kingdom over their own.

I want to keep this healthy perspective of money. I want to be a good steward and no longer chase money, but chase the ministry God gives me. To be used by God when, where, and how He wants to use me – but if I'm too distracted chasing money, I may miss these opportunities, just like the rich young ruler did.

The next step in developing our financial stewardship is related to our prioritization of money. This is directly driven by our perspective. For if we look to money, more than God, then we prioritize it into the position of an idol. It basically becomes our god.

PRIORITIZATION

Money can never be our primary motivator and priority. That is where so many of us go wrong. We convince ourselves it's not, but in the end, money is what we are most consumed with. We want more of it, we stress over it, we think it is the answer to our problems, we think those who have a lot of it are somehow superior to those with less. None of these assumptions are true of course, and they tend to position money in a place it doesn't belong.

Clearly, the Bible teaches the value of good planning, and that involves proper prioritization. Ecclesiastes and Proverbs for example, are filled with wisdom principals. The best planning always involves execution and application. An example of this is seen in Proverbs 28:19, where we are told how "those who work their land will have abundant food, but those who chase fantasies will have their fill of poverty."

This isn't a promise that we will always be rich and never have struggle, but it is a principal that encourages us to mix our faith and work together. They go hand in hand. We do our best, give God our best, seek to be obedient to Him, and then trust Him with the outcomes.

The problem is many of us don't know and have never learned how to properly handle money. It's like being given land and told to start growing crops. We may have never learned how to farm and are now expected to do so.

Likewise, we get money, but never learn how to use it most effectively. So, perhaps we begin to covet it, squander it, etc. I didn't know how to manage it effectively at first, and even though the financial industry offers some valuable lessons, the opinions vary greatly. It can be difficult to muddle through all the data.

Ultimately, the Bible offers the clarity we need. We then seek to apply the financial strategies that best compliment the Biblical outline provided.

As a result, this empowers our ability to customize a solid financial plan. For money is now properly prioritized in our life as a tool and resource – not the "source" to all our hopes and desires.

I eventually came to a place in my life where I realized my priorities were all mixed up. I said I believed in God, but didn't do anything much beyond saying it. I said I loved my family, but wasn't involved to the extend love calls us to. The same contradiction was there with money. I had become blinded to the reality that all my hope was placed in it.

What do we place our hope in? Is it other people? Do we hope others will like us and if they do, we will be better off? Or, is our hope in our job and career? What if it goes away? Is our hope in our family? Or, is our hope in our money, and do we trust it as our source of provision and protection more than God?

Quite simply, for me, prioritization is a matter of what my heart most hopes in. When we place our hope in anything – anything, besides Jesus Christ, we are standing on shaky ground. However, when our hopes are in Christ, and we realize He is our Source, all these other "things" fall into place. They are resources provided by Him. We are the stewards of our finances, family, health, and as mentioned, our measure of faith.

By approaching the issue of money with this heart and mindset, we are now positioned to begin the proper preparations that include establishing our spending, saving and giving plans.

PREPARATIONS: SPENDING PLAN

We all spend money, but how we spend it varies greatly - some are frugal, some wasteful, some flamboyant and some responsible. Our goal is to get in the responsible category. So, let's look at how we spend our money. Clearly, this involves having a budget, but there's more to it. We can budget how much our expenses are each month, how much in eating out and entertainment we will allow, but there is also how we structure debts, save on expenses and reduce our overall costs. For this all impacts our spending.

Early in my marriage, my wife will be the first to tell you, I was clueless with our finances. I hate to admit that, but it's true. I couldn't balance a check book to save my life, and my wife had to eventually take over - embarrassing to admit.

It wasn't until I got deep into the financial industry that light bulbs starting going off in my mind. I was finally learning about money, how it works, how to manage it, and what not to do.

I quickly began applying these insights and our financial situation slowly turned around. In fact, as I will disclose in later chapters, the pendulum swung way too far the other direction and I went from barely thinking about money to nearly obsessing over it – poor prioritization!

As with everything, there is a proper balance, and I want to share these lessons acquired over time.

This information may be brand new to some and old school for others, but either way, perhaps some of the testimonies shared intermittently will prove helpful to all.

We will begin our tactical training by getting a better understanding of financial institutions.

Why? Because millions of people have deposit accounts, mortgages, credit cards, and/or some other type of banking service. So, it makes sense to get a better understanding of these places, and how to best utilize their services and partner with them.

Financial Partnerships

As stated, the first step in maximizing our financial relations is to understand our partner. In this case, the partner is the financial industry.

To begin, most financial institutions develop a

niche. For example, this may mean some lenders want to cater to real estate investors, farmers, medical professionals, etc.

Therefore, step 1 is to find out your financial organization's niche and if your need fits it.

The Perfect Match

Are you what your partner is looking for? In other words, are you a perfect match, or customer? If not, that's okay, you can get around it, but first, you must know where you stand. So, what is the perfect customer?

In essence, it is similar for the majority of financial institutions out there. Simplified, it's the individual and/or business seeking loans, deposits and investments, but more importantly, it's the customer with cash flow, liquidity and healthy beacon scores.

Take loans for example, quite simply, lenders want to approve as many deals as they can. After all, that's one way they make money, but you must remember, they are regulated and audited by the government so they have to be careful with how aggressive they get. So, they love the "slam dunks," which basically is the person with a beacon score over 680 and a steady income stream.

A **beacon score**, also known as a credit score, is determined by three major companies, Equifax, Experian, and TransUnion. They monitor all of your loans, also known as **credits**, and track how many times you are late with your payments and your credit balances. The higher your score the better! If you have late pays and a lot of maxed-out credit cards, this can lower your score.

Lower credit scores can greatly decrease your financial options and increase your fees and interest rates due to a presumed increase in credit risk. The lower credit market is defined as **subprime**. We want to do our best to keep you out of this segment and keep you in the prime segment because this is where the best deals are made!

So, the best way to keep your score up is to make your payments on time and to keep your credit card balances as low as possible. This is a simplistic approach, but it works. Some other tips include, avoid opening numerous credit accounts and having too many credit inquires pulled. A credit check is performed any time you try to qualify for a loan, or new credit.

If you'd like additional information on credit reports, you can visit equifax.com, transunion.com and experian.com.

Naturally, if there's a perfect customer, there must also be a worst customer. Who's that? Basically, the worst customer is most likely the same as your worst customer. Which most likely is someone who is irate, unreasonable, high tempered, and rude.

The #1 rule in working with any financial firm goes back to the basics of life – you get more with "honey than vinegar". This means you win more often with kindness than with negative behavior. No one likes dealing with rude people. In fact, time and again, the polite customer gets what they want more often than the person yelling.

I will never understand why "rude" people think this is how to get what they want. They remind me of the child throwing a temper tantrum on the floor, kicking their feet and hands. I promise you will get more financial privileges and more out of life, if you use kindness, in lieu of anger.

Finance 101 – Know Your Partner

To have a working relationship you must

understand what makes your partner tick. So, let's learn some of the basics of the financial industry.

Did you know most financial institutions view loans, as assets, or sources of income? And that they consider interest bearing deposits, such as savings accounts, as liabilities, or outflows of cash? When you think about it, it makes sense. They have to pay you interest on your savings account, which costs money. However, you pay interest on your loan, thus they make money.

Another source of income for many companies is generated through fees. As you know, there are overdraft fees, minimum balance fees, check card fees and etc. In fact, fees are a huge source of income. So, if you're someone that bounces checks and constantly spends more than you have in your checking account – you're paying much more to a bank than you have to.

Then of course there are loan fees, another strong source of direct income – most often this is 1 percent of the loan amount.

There are naturally other ways money is generated in the financial industry, but for the most part and for simplicity, fees and interest payments are the major sources.

Please note that big companies and smaller companies may charge different fees and have different niches. For example, many of the big firms don't charge fees for a check card, or online services and electronic bill pay. However, some of the smaller community institutions do. At the same time, some community organizations may provide more customization in lending money since they are based locally.

So, what have we learned so far? Know your finance company's niche and what makes a good customer. It's that simple, but you will be amazed at how far this insight can take you. It is the basis and foundation all the other insights work from. You must have this one down first and then all the others work more effectively.

Now that you know who makes the best customer and worst customer and how revenue is generated, let's dissect this information further to uncover additional financial insights.

Maximize your cash

One of the best ways to make money is by saving

money. So, let's learn how to reduce some of those fees we just discussed and how to possibly get rid of them all together.

Fees

As shared earlier, fees are a source of income, but for those in the know, they can be avoided, or reduced significantly.

I'm also going to educate you on fees you may not have known ever existed. The so-called "hidden" fees or the fees you always expected to pay.

Overdraft fees tend to be the largest fees of all. They can be as much as $50 per overdraft! The saddest part is I've seen countless individuals have five checks clear at once, without the funds available, because a deposit wasn't made in time. You can do the math, but that's a $250 fee! So, what can you do to avoid them?

First, get overdraft protection. This can sometimes be set up on a credit card, home equity line-of-credit, or linked to another account. No matter how you set it up, get it. It can save you thousands of dollars. If you can't get overdraft for some reason, you may get all, or a portion of your fees refunded if you ask, but it's going to be based upon the reason you went into overdraft. Again, use kindness and do your best to never have it happen again.

Service fees for statements, money orders, and check cashing services can almost always be avoided, especially if you maintain a checking, savings, investment and/or lending relationship with the company. These fees are typically no larger than $5. So, simply ask how you can avoid these fees in the future. Typically, you can link multiple accounts together, transfer additional funds over, or simply upgrade your account to accomplish this.

Now, pay close attention - I'm about to share one of the most crucial elements to maximizing your money. It's definitely an easy and best kept secret most don't realize. It is a painfully obvious tactic, and the ones' that know it, use it well and use it to their advantage daily! What is it? Again, it's a simple tool you can start using immediately to your advantage. Starting tomorrow, get to know and build a relationship with someone in the organization. That's it!

Typically, most people simply make account

deposits and loan payments and hardly ever think about additional money matters unless they have a problem to resolve. They pay their fees and simply take things at face value, but those that slow down and take the time to build a relationship with someone in the company win deals you would love to be a part of!

Now, the individual ideally needs to have some authority, such as a manager, or some other platform associate, preferably in sales (**platform** is jargon for employees that don't work behind teller lines). Usually, the sales people that do loans, deposits and investments, as well as the branch managers are the best ones to get to know. They're the ones most likely doing the negotiations anyway - thus, the importance of building relationships with them. It doesn't take much either, simply learn their name, or send a thank you card. The smallest gesture can go a long way to winning your negotiations and increasing your profits!

So, concerning many of the fees mentioned, avoiding them is where your relationship comes in to play, and your new friend will be there to help when needed.

Some other fees you may not be as aware of include, check card fees, and online bill pay fees. You should rarely have to pay these. There are far too many organizations that offer these features free.

Concerning one more insight about debit cards, did you know the finance company makes money each time you swipe your card? The payout can vary based upon whether you swipe it as a credit card, or debit card on the machine. It doesn't make a difference to you at all, the money still comes out of your account no matter which option you choose, credit, or debit, but it makes a nice difference to the company your card is with.

What are some other fees you can avoid? By simply asking and perhaps linking a few of your accounts together, or by consolidating accounts from other financial institutions, you may rid yourself of safety deposit box fees, low balance fees, and deposit activity fees.

Deposit activity and balance fees are charges applied when your balance drops below a set limit and when your deposits and withdrawals exceed a set limit. Again, these can typically be avoided by upgrading your account, linking accounts, and/or moving accounts from another institution.

I'd like to re-emphasize your finance company is in business to make money and typically make fee refunds and offer higher interest rates for those that have accounts with them, can bring more accounts to them and/or have other financial needs, such as loans and investments. They won't just do these adjustments for everyone, every time - nor should they.

Even better news is how easy it is to gain these benefits. All of which improve your financial IQ!

The deeper we get, the more knowledge you will gain in finances – and become more empowered to establish the basic habits necessary to be a better steward of your money.

Understanding Leverage

I have been working in the financial industry for quite a while and am often asked by fellow Christians what my opinion on debt is. Nowhere does the Bible say debt is a sin, but it does indicate it can be dangerous and therefore, we must understand how to properly utilize it (Proverbs 22:7). It's sad to see people get in so much debt they can barely breathe, but with responsible borrowing, it can be paid down, used to serve a purpose, and be a win-win for all.

The secret of using leverage correctly and understanding the strategy and power behind using **OPM**, or other peoples' money, is a valuable insight. Often times this powerful concept is shared from the perspective of the borrower, which is fine, but what I'm about to share with you is the view point of the one holding the money.

In addition, you will have the power of understanding the mind of the lender. You will know what they are looking for and their thought process. This provides you with confidence, but more than that, it puts the lender at ease and builds their confidence with you, which allows them the comfort of saying yes more often.

Again, I'll cover both residential and commercial lending, but first, let's address the basics shared by both types of credit – pricing and amortization options.

Residential Loan Concepts

Understanding your pricing and amortization

options and the benefits they provide allows you to maximize your wealth strategy and put it in overdrive. You need to know when to choose one loan over the other, and you need to know why to do it. Again, knowledge is power and the key to effective money management.

Let's begin by discussing your pricing and loan structure options. Basically, you have two pricing models, or rates to choose from - fixed, or variable. You also have two loan structures to choose from - interest only and amortizing. Knowing when to use one over the other is crucial to maximizing your profits. Thus, winning with leverage. You begin to implement control over money, not the other way around.

Remember, companies are in business to make money, and rightfully so, and lenders are some of the best, almost by default. For example, when the economy experiences a decline in rates, people tend to rush out to fix their variable rates and begin to accumulate more debt, or buy more. When rates begin to climb, people rush to lock in their variable rates and decide to make the big purchases they waited to buy when rates were lower to avoid even higher rates.

Basically, people will always have a need to borrow money. This is especially true in America – we love debt! It seems we don't know what to do without it. Sadly, most people let money control them and are prisoners of debt. I want to empower you to be the commander of your money and to learn how to use it as a tool, not a crutch. Interestingly, one key to this strategy is doing the opposite of what the mass public does.

In other words, borrow variable debt, or establish lines of credit when you don't need the money. Also, you want to term out, or fix any debt that you plan to hold long-term.

Again, this is in contrast to most people that rush at the last minute to get loans as they need them and use variable lines-of-credit incorrectly for long-term purposes.

Why establish a line-of-credit when you don't need it? Because you'll be ready to make financial moves fast! The thing to remember about LOCs is that they are for short-term usage, opportunities, and emergencies.

For example, let's say you're a real estate investor and learn of a piece of property going up for sale.

The property is in a prime location and has excellent tenants. So, you know the property will go quickly when it's advertised to the public, but you don't have the cash available to buy it. You need a loan, but the lender is requesting income verification and has to do title and flood searches. At best, they need two days to approve your loan, but you don't have two days to wait.

Unfortunately, while you were visiting your financing company, someone else wrote a check to the seller of your dream investment property shortly after hearing of the opportunity. This individual was prepared and you lost because you weren't.

Let's now assume you have $20k in cash earning a strong interest rate in a savings account. So, you don't want to spend a dime of it. However, you find a great deal on a car you know you can resell for a profit. The car is selling for $20k and needs some work. You know you can do the repairs and resell the car for $40k, but again, you don't want to use your cash. What do you do? You use your LOC, make the repairs, sell the car and make $20k in one month with just $34 out of pocket! How? Easy – you employ the power of strategic leverage!

Assume your LOC has a variable rate of Prime, which let's say equals 6 percent at the time. This rate charged to a $20k balance works out to be $100 interest-only. And since you let your money earn, let's say, 4 percent interest, your $20k pays you roughly $66 in interest a month. So, basically, you invested $34, the difference between $100 and $66, and earned $20k. All this assuming you resold the car in one month! Not bad!

Now, just imagine doing this with larger deals. The money can add up fast. Again, this is the ideal way to use variable rate, interest-only LOCs to your advantage.

This concept even works with CDs. Did you know you can collateralize a loan with a CD? You can, which as the previous car example illustrates, reduces the actual interest rate you end up paying. Meaning the interest earned from the CD offsets the interest charged on the loan. Again maximizing your return and maximizing the power of leverage! You can also use this strategy with brokerage/investment accounts as well.

Concerning using LOCs in case of emergencies, let's say your car's transmission decides to fail. Now, you have to replace it, but don't want to use your cash. Or, you have home repairs you need to make. The list of emergencies is as long as the list for opportunities. Thus, a benefit of LOCs.

Now, how about amortized loans with fixed rates? How do you use these to your advantage?

Amortized, or fixed payment loans are best for long-term purchases. Using the same real estate example mentioned earlier, let's assume you put forth your new knowledge and established a $100k LOC before you needed it. You were able to negotiate the sales price of the property down from $120k to $95k simply by offering to pay cash that day! As a side note, you immediately make a $25k profit, again by having your LOC ready.

However, since you know you're going to hold this property long-term to benefit from the $800 monthly rental check coming in, you decide to lock your variable rate and pay off the balance on your LOC - which by the way, allows you to reuse your $100k LOC at a later time. You negotiate an 80 percent loan-to-value fixed rate loan for 30 years, at let's assume, 5.5 percent. This makes your monthly payment before taxes and insurance, $537.

The result? This investment and loan structuring

allows you to make a monthly profit of $263 (monthly rent minus monthly mortgage). Thus, the power of knowing when and how to use pricing and loan structuring to your advantage!

Within a few paragraphs, you just learned some tactics to help you better control money, rather than having it control you.

Before we continue, we need to make sure some basic concepts are understood so that you have all the tools necessary to maximize your potential with each insight revealed.

For example, rates can currently be based on Prime, or LIBOR and lines-of-credit can have fixed rates and amortized loans can be interest-only.

Prime Rate is defined by The Wall Street Journal as "The base rate on corporate loans posted by at least 75% of the nation's 30 largest banks".[5]

LIBOR is an abbreviation for the "London Interbank Offered Rate," and is the interest rate offered by a specific group of London banks for U.S. dollar deposits of a stated maturity.

Both Prime and LIBOR are used as a base index for setting rates on various credit options.

Most often there isn't much benefit going with one index over the other. It's true that LIBOR is typically lower than Prime, but lenders get around that by usually adding a larger spread to their LIBOR based credits. So, you end up with basically the same rate either way.

For example, if Prime is 7 percent and LIBOR is 5 percent then the lender may offer you a LOC priced at Prime plus 1 percent, or LIBOR plus 3 percent. So, don't be too impressed with someone's LIBOR based loan, they most likely are paying the same rate ultimately as your PRIME based loan.

So, why do a fixed loan over a line-of-credit? Again, it's about understanding the best leverage for your strategy. Is the money borrowed going to be used for long-term or short-term purposes? A more important question is do you know the best time to borrow long-term, or short-term? The answers to these questions vary per situation and some answers may surprise you.

Did you realize that the average homeowner in the United States stays in their house between 7 and 9 years? At the same time, many Americans have 30 year fixed mortgages on their homes.

Okay, here's the question - Why would you want to pay interest on a 30 year term if you most likely won't live in your home for 30 years? It doesn't make sense in this case. For example, if you're 35 years old and just got a 30 year fixed loan, you will be 65 years old before the loan is paid off! Again, that's even if you stay in the house that long. Remember, the average person moves every 7 to 9 years.

Did you also know that the typical 30 year fixed mortgage is structured so that you pay primarily interest for the first 15 years? Almost 84 percent of your monthly payment goes straight to interest. A very small portion goes to reduce the principal. So, what does this all mean? Well, for starters, you can end up paying far more than the loan amount by the time your 30 year loan is paid off.

Boiled down, if you know you're not going to stay in a home greater than 15 years, you may want to consider getting an interest only loan and pay over your billed amount. Why? Your monthly payments are lower compared to a conventional 30 year note and you can reduce your principal debt quicker if you pay over what your interest-only bill is.

Let's illustrate this further. Let's say you purchase a

$300k home and put 20 percent down. So, your first mortgage is $240k. Now, let's assume you get a conventional 30 year mortgage at a rate of 6.5 percent. This makes your monthly payment, without taxes and insurance included, roughly $1517. The same payment on an interest only loan at 6.5 percent is $1300. That's a $200 savings per month! Of course 30 year and interest only rates differ, but for simplicity purposes, we used the same rate.

Now, let's assume you have an interest-only loan and pay over the $1300. You decide to pay the same amount you would be paying if you had a conventional 30 year. This has you paying roughly $217 a month straight to your principal, which immediately increases your equity. A conventional note doesn't do that. Remember, your payment goes mostly to interest for approximately the first 15 years.

Am I against conventional loans and totally for interest only? Absolutely not! Remember, I'm simply sharing different strategies and insights. This is simply another tool in your financial arsenal to implement, if appropriate. You need to be aware of your options and the whys behind your financial decisions.

Again, most people are going to obtain debt sometime during their life. If you can avoid it – good, but most likely you may find a time you need to take out a loan. It's during these times, I want to help you be wiser, and not foolish. Debt can be very dangerous, but even a little know-how can help save you from future financial troubles and struggles down the road.

As we continue, your loan choices are numerous when it comes to mortgages. There are one month, one year, three year, five year and many, many more interest only options, but the list is equally long when it comes to conventional or traditional type loans.

For example, you can get five year, ten year, fifteen year, twenty year and of course thirty year fixed rate loans. Then, there are adjustable rate mortgages with rates that are variable, or fluctuate with the Prime and/or LIBOR indexes.

With so many choices it's easy to see why so many people get confused and stressed and therefore seek professional guidance. Hopefully, most of the time the guidance sought is truthful and in your best interest, but I want to help teach you some tips that will help you feel less vulnerable and dependent upon others. I want to make sure you are better prepared with your financial insights to help you walk away from loan closings feeling empowered, not beaten.

Do you currently know how to decide which mortgage product is best for you?

The one with the lowest rate and that best fits your need of course! It's that easy. You simply need to understand what your need is – that's the tough part.

Are you buying an investment property that you plan to rent long-term, or sell immediately? If you plan to hold and payoff long-term, perhaps the 30 year note will work best. It provides security from any surprises in rate and allows you to adjust your incoming rent to ensure a profit. However, if you plan to sell the property fast, perhaps a variable and interest only loan will work best by allowing you the lowest monthly payments possible. Thus reducing your expenses until you can resell.

Do you feel like you may most likely move again within 7 to 9 years? If so, perhaps a 10 year interest only would work best, allowing you a lower monthly payment as compared to the conventional 30 year. This may also help you generate more equity through debt/principal reduction and depend less on market appreciation.

I think you get the idea. The key is first think about your future. What are you going to do? What do you plan to do? What would you like to do? Then choose.

To ensure you get the best deal on your loans, keep in mind, you get more when you have more. For example, grocery stores may offer a free loaf of bread when you purchase two. Similarly, if you're looking to get a loan, the company you're dealing with may offer discounts and better rates to those with multiple products with them. Why? Well, if they have your checking, your savings, your loans, your investments, and your insurance, then they make money on all of it. Therefore, they may consider giving up a little on an additional product being offered than risk losing what you already have with them.

You may be one who prefers to spread your money around town and not have too much at the same place. You don't want to keep all your eggs in one basket. The theory is that if you spread it around, you risk less and you build relations with several institutions. Not a bad idea, but in a time when every business wants to be your one-stop shop, you get benefits if you play their game. Keep in mind the more you offer to bring over, the more discounts and benefits you'll likely get and should get.

So, how does commercial lending work and how can you ensure yourself the best deal in the small business world? Read on.

Small Business Concepts

Few retail lenders, much less consumers, have a high comfort level when it comes to commercial lending. In fact, many retail lenders quiver at the thought of doing commercial loans. Ironically, the opposite tends to be true of commercial lenders – some cringe at consumer lending. Fortunately, you are learning key insights to both distinctly different areas, allowing you to become all the more wiser in the long run.

Why does commercial lending seem to intimidate and confuse so many? I guess because often times the numbers are bigger. The deposits are bigger, the transactions are more numerous and the loans are definitely bigger, but basically, a loan is a loan and a deposit is deposit and there's not much need to be intimidated by commercial lending.

It's important to note that the same rules apply. You get more benefits if you have more business relationships with the finance company, and if you're nice to deal with.

Many commercial lenders have the reputation of being extremely picky about whom they lend money to. They naturally tend to prefer dealing with the crème-de-la-crème of businesses and business owners. Granted, that's good for the lender, but can leave some business owners out in the cold and without a loan. So, we need to make sure you present yourself as good as possible when dealing with commercial lenders.

What's the best of the best look like in the small business world? Want to be one? Then read on, and learn how to have the commercial lenders eating out of your hand.

Cash flow, credit and collateral – that's basically it! That is what you need the majority of the time to get approved for a commercial loan - cash flow to repay your debt, good credit scores, and the collateral to cover it. Not really rocket science, but getting the best rate and terms can sometimes feel as difficult.

Let's illustrate this point further.

The Five C's Of Credit

As you know by now, a good way to ensure you're getting the best deal is to know what a lender is looking for. For commercial customers, many times this is what's called **the 5-Cs of credit**, or the five key elements a borrower should have to obtain credit. We already listed three, but here's the full list: character (integrity), capacity (sufficient cash flow to service the obligation), capital (net worth), collateral (assets to secure the debt), and conditions (the current state of borrower and economy).

Now, let's examine each element separately.

Character - What's your integrity like? How do you treat your employees and customers? What's your personal and your company's reputation like in the industry and community? How do you handle your responsibilities and fulfill your obligations?

Obviously credit, or beacon score is one tool

lenders use to help evaluate character. For example, do you pay your bills on time, or even at all? Bottom line...in business as in life, your character and how well you handle your affairs affects what you get in return. In other words, you reap what you sow.

Capacity – Do you have enough money to pay back the debt you're seeking? How much debt can your company handle?

Lenders look at debt coverage ratios, along with other ratios, as tools to help determine capacity. Naturally, some lenders have more aggressive ratios than others. For example, a **DSC**, or a debt service coverage ratio of 1.25 can be simplified to roughly illustrate that you have $1.25 of revenue coming in for every $1 of outgoing debt. This DSC ratio is determined by dividing the lender's projected net operating income by the loan debt service.

Amazingly, I've seen some lenders make loans with 1.0 DSC ratios! I've also seen very conservative lenders require a minimum of 1.80 DSC. Again, it all depends on the personality of the organization you're dealing with. So, don't be too discouraged if you're turned down by one firm. Ask why you were turned down and what your DSC ratio was. This will better help you shop your request at another financial institution.

Capital – What's your company's net worth? How much money have you put back in your business?

Both your company's financial statements and your personal credit are crucial elements to addressing capital. For example, if your company has a negative net worth, are you prepared to add more of your own money, if needed? Can your personal resources support both you and the business as it is growing? If your company has not yet made money, then a strong personal financial statement and payment history may help offset this issue.

Collateral – What do you have to put up as a secondary source of repayment for your loan, if you were to fail on your monthly debt payments?

Many finance groups tend to be cash flow lenders. Meaning, they look for their primary source of repayment to be from your current cash flow, but they also want a back-up plan. This is where your collateral comes in. Most collateral is a hard asset, or something tangible such as real estate, car, boat, cash, certificates of deposit, equipment and/or inventory. Your company's accounts receivables may also be used.

A point on collateral is a percentage of its value is used to establish your loan amount. Also, personal collateral, such as your primary residence can be used to help establish commercial loans and LOCs.

Conditions – Simply, what is the current state of your company, yourself and the economy? For example, how does your business perform during a recessionary period? What are the trends of your company's industry? Are you currently going through a messy divorce? Basically, how are you, your business and the economy doing overall and how are each impacted by the other?

Even though each element of the 5-Cs is important, they don't carry equal weighting with lenders. It's a balancing act and one element may help offset a weaker element and vice versa. For example, you may have a low personal credit score because of the amount of revolving debt you have outstanding. However, your company's strong cash flow and collateral can help offset the low beacon and get you the loan. Also, remember, that one weighting of the 5-Cs may differ from another company. So, know your strengths and weaknesses in each area and be prepared to promote them for the best deal. This also goes back to an initial insight learned about knowing your lender's niche.

The secret of the 5-Cs is powerful. Why? Because, you know what the lender is looking for and you know what to highlight. You also know where you stand. As I keep repeating, the key to winning is first understanding the game. You can now look through a lender's eye and have insight to what they look for.

Getting back to niche, you also know that some lenders focus on different strengths, or elements. Some organizations out there are collateral lenders and don't look at the cash flow as much as others. Some focus on cash flow the most, but again, the ratios vary from lender to lender. That's why you need to know your organization's niche. You may be at the wrong institution to fulfill your needs. It's like wearing shoes too small – it hurts! Sadly, it hurts your pocket the most and can prevent you from maximizing your wealth and company's growth.

E.B.I.T.D.A.

Now that you understand the 5-Cs, let's assume

you're concerned about your cash flow and want to know a little more about it. Since this is such an important part of the process, let me share with you a simple insight you may not be aware of. Your cash flow may be better than you think. Let's first look at a quick diagnosis you can perform using your company's tax returns that will allow you to quickly determine if you even have enough business cash flow available to get the loan you want.

This quick insight is known as EBITDA, and it's a tool used often in underwriting processes, but I want you to understand what it is and how you can use it to better understand what lenders look for.

EBITDA is Earnings Before Interest, Taxes, Depreciation and Amortization. It is determined using the following calculation:

> Net Income minus Operating Expenses equals Operating Profit (EBIT). Now, add back Depreciation Expense and Amortization Expense. This equals EBITDA!
>
> (Net income – Operating expense) + Depreciation + Amortization = EBITDA

Underwriters may also add back officer salary and rent payments. So, when all these add backs are made, your net income may be greatly improved. Thus, your cash flow could be better than you initially thought.

Another interesting use of EBITDA is that it can be used as a rough, and I emphasize the word rough, way to calculate what your business may be worth on the open market. Again, these rough estimates can give you an idea of what you may potentially sell your business for. Please note however, that the use of a professional CPA or other evaluation firm is a must to properly place a value on your business, but for a loose translation this EBITDA tool may help. Quite simply, calculate your company's EBITDA and then multiply it five to seven times. This is the estimated valuation range for your business.

Okay, now that you understand some basic forms of underwriting and tools of the trade, what good is it? Well, now you can have a better understanding of your business financials and your banker, and by understanding these things you're better prepared to have more productive conversations with your lender.

Commercial Loan Options

There isn't much flavor when it comes to commercial loan options. It's basically vanilla and chocolate. You won't find any fancy flavors here. Unlike consumer loans, where you can get 100 percent and higher loan-to-values, as well as 30 year amortizations, commercial lending is much more conservative. Typically, at best, you find 20 year amortizations and 5 to 15 year fixed rate options in commercial lending.

Basically, unless you're getting multi-million dollar loans with rate swaps, your loan options will most likely be:

- 5 year fixed rates with a maximum 20 year amortization.

- 15 year fixed rates on a 15 year amortization.

- Variable rate loans, renewable every year.

In addition, loan-to-values tend to be conservative. Most commercial lenders like to stay at 80 percent LTV on real estate and equipment deals, 65 percent on raw land, 75 percent on accounts receivable and 80 percent on inventory.

Of course, as in retail, CD, brokerage and cash collateralized loans exist in the small business world and also range in loan-to-value percentages.

Now, naturally, there is some variety in the market place; and as I've mentioned, many organizations have a niche which allow them to make enhancements to their products, but for the most part, the standard options listed are what you typically find. There are interest-only loans and lines-of-credit, and as mentioned, rate swaps for larger credits.

What are **rate swaps**? They allow you greater flexibility on loan terms, but generally come with a fee and are separate contracts. In fact, some firms don't offer rate swaps, or derivatives. It's usually reserved for the larger institutions. However, if you're curious, deals typically over one million can get a derivative contract added to their loan contract. This derivative contract can allow you to fix your rate for longer terms and allow for longer amortization schedules. For example, one can potentially get a thirty year fixed rate loan, or better, when the standard commercial amortization is only twenty years.

So, now that you are armed with the basic

knowledge needed to get the right loan for you at the best terms, you can decide to shop all the lenders yourself for a winning deal, or hire someone to do all the leg work for you. If you go with someone else, that most likely is a loan broker, and it's important you fully understand the way they work too. Again, knowledge is power.

Loan Brokers

Why would you hire someone to shop the best loan for your business, and for that matter, for your personal needs? One reason is that it can save you time. If you're running a full time business and don't have much time, but want to get the best deal possible, or if you know you have some obstacles to overcome and your business may not fit into typical underwriting policies, then you may benefit by seeking a qualified and credible loan broker.

Brokers are middle men. Their clients seek their services to have them shop a variety of financial institutions to find the best deal available for their business, or personal situation. Brokers can find you a home mortgage and commercial mortgage, but many specialize in one area over another. Brokers make their money by charging a fee and/or getting paid by the lender they shop your loan to.

You may have never heard of a loan broker and if you have, you may have a negative image of them in your mind.

There are good and bad brokers just like there are good and bad doctors. It's all up to you as to who you get – be picky, but also know what to ask for.

Make sure you fully understand how the broker makes their money. Also, make sure there are no hidden fees. Brokers can sometimes offer you a higher rate than what is being offered by the lender to make a spread. Thus, the higher the broker increases the offered rate, the more money they make. Avoid this situation. Make sure you're getting the rate being offered by the financial institution shopped without the broker tacking on an extra spread. Also, if you can, try to find a broker that doesn't charge you an upfront fee. Don't pay a dime, until you get a loan approval that you agree to and feel comfortable with.

Also, keep in mind, when you shop several loans, your credit is pulled by each lender and this can negatively affect your bureau score. The more inquiries done on you, the lower your score can go.

So, be careful. This is true even if you decide to shop your own loan. Each lender is going to "pull" your credit. Therefore, I suggest you try to limit your shops to one big lender and one small one. Also, ask around. Ask other business owners where they got their loan and how the process went and what terms were offered. If you're turned down by both lenders you may consider a loan broker to help you source other options.

You may have to pay a higher rate to get your loan, but make sure you fully understand the rate and fees you're being offered. Most often, the broker doesn't get paid until after you get your money, or at the closing. You may even be able to pay your broker fee with your loan proceeds.

Congratulations – you're progressing nicely and by reading this far, you now know more financial insights than the average person! You possess an empowered financial IQ allowing you to develop enriching partnerships, maximize money and control the power of leverage, rather than having debt control you.

Now we're ready to address and reveal strategies involving investments.

As you know, investment management is offered most everywhere and there are so many choices. So, it's crucial to learn what to look for and how to win with your advisor, as well as in the market. Are you ready? Then let's maximize your wealth IQ even more!

SAVINGS PLAN

Now that we have learned some insights affecting our spending plan, hopefully, we can take some of that learning and apply our new found money to our savings.

Sadly, many articles have been written about how little people save in general and have set aside for retirement. In addition, others don't have enough insurance, a will, medical directive, and/or a trust in place to best protect their families in case of death, or illness. Savings is basically planning ahead.

We are also told in 2 Kings 4 how a widow was left in a difficult financial situation after her husband died. He is described as a man who knew God and served Him. Therefore, we can assume he was a righteous and Godly man. However, he clearly left his family in debt and without any effective planning in place.

Unfortunately, this story paints a picture that is far too true for many families. Good people – and Christian people, who fail to implement sound financial stewardship. Clearly, we don't know all the reasons this man in the Bible left his family in this situation, but for us, we can learn from it and begin to do all the things necessary to protect and care for those we love. The problem however is procrastination. We falsely assume we have time.

I personally recall a situation when a wealthy land owner died unexpectedly. He was a very loving man, but he left his family with very little liquidity to pay the remaining debts they had. He had planned to take care of this, but of course, he died before he could get to it. Therefore, his family was faced with the added stress of having to decide which assets to sell in order to pay their debts.

Again, effective planning can help address much of this, but we must take action. We must not delay. We must take care of business and get a will, start saving, get a medical directive, and have a plan for emergencies.

Proverbs 6:8 directs us to look at the ant and how even it stores provisions without anyone telling it to. Thus, we should be all the more wiser with our preparations. So let's get started.

Emergency Savings

Not too long ago our heating and air system went out. Unfortunately, to get things running again, we were told we needed new units. They even showed us the burned out unit. So, I believed them. Then the bill came, and it was a doozy. Thankfully, we didn't have to go in debt to pay for it and thankfully, we had the cash to pay for the replacement, because of our emergency fund.

This is just one example as to why having an emergency fund is so important, but so many folks simply don't have one. So, when emergencies come up, they face some serious challenges. Now, I realize building an emergency fund can be difficult, especially when money is tight, but getting in the habit of putting a portion of money aside is extremely valuable.

Having at least 3 months living expenses set aside is a good target to have and having 12 months is best. You may be laughing at the thought of having 12 months reserve put aside, but let me share a powerful testimony in this regard.

As we know, big companies and some small ones, periodically go through downsizing, I have had my fair share of them. There were periods when I never truly knew how long I was going to have a job. This uncertainty proved helpful though, because it forced me to save when times were good and the money was flowing. So, my wife and I avoided the temptation many fall into when more money is made. We did not go out and buy new cars. We did not put in the new pool. We did not buy the vacation home. Again, none of those things are wrong, but they should not be pursued in lieu of first establishing an emergency fund.

During one of the corporate transitions, one of my highest paying jobs suddenly took a different direction and I was asked to take on a different role. The role being positioned to me did not interest me at all for various reasons and so I initially said no, but this literally left me without a job. My wife thought I was crazy at first and so I began to second guess myself, but by that time the job was off the table. Now, I was faced with finding another position.

I initially didn't think this would take long, but soon found out good jobs are hard to come by.

The good news is I could afford to take my time and not take the first jobs that came my way. In fact, I turned several down.

In addition, it was during this time, I felt led to go on my first international mission trip to South Africa for nearly two weeks. Again - no job.

I also took this time to write my children's book, *STRONG and the Kingdom Scrolls* and finalize my novel, *Highways End*.

I continued to go on job interviews and after about seven months passed, I had two job offers I was very interested in. I will go into how I chose between those two in a later chapter, but for now, the point is our emergency savings helped us during this transition.

My wife could continue to homeschool our kids, we could still pay our bills, I could go on a mission trip, write a book, and prayerfully seek the position I felt God wanted me to take. Just imagine being able to select the person and the company you "want" to work for rather than "have" to work for? That is truly a blessed gift!

Again, this is the power of not spending everything

we make, and establishing savings, especially when times are good. Avoid the temptation to spend more. Instead, save more - but don't hoard it.

Those 7 months were like a Sabbath. It was truly a spiritual journey of seeing God's faithfulness prove true because I was faithful with His money.

Money seems to be like the ocean tide, and we can see this with the stock market. There are ups and there are downs. There are high tides and low tides - times money flows in and times money seems to flow out. We must plan on this - expect this and plan for this. So, do not negate your emergency savings, and get started any way you can, but get started and begin putting money away for those rainy days that are sure to come.

Long Term Savings & Investments

I personally believe investments are part of a long term savings strategy, which is why I have them lumped together. Long term savings include our retirement goals, as well as all those other financial goals we have down the road, like paying for our kids' college(s), wedding(s), etc.

To me, these are our dreams, but to make these

dreams a reality, it takes work, sacrifice and wisdom.

I have unfortunately discovered however that many people have stopped dreaming. It was during a speaking engagement we do at work this realization was made vivid. Members of my team were talking about the importance of saving and pursuing goals, but members of the audience confessed they were in such dire financial stress, they couldn't afford to dream. They were in survival mode. Simply, trying to make ends meet. They had bills to pay, kids to feed, and pursuing their dreams was something they left behind with childhood.

Some of us can relate. We are told dreaming is childish. We get in survival mode, but I believe dreaming can be a very powerful motivator. We must not give up on our dreams. For they help prosper hope, motivation, and propel action.

When speaking to groups on financial literacy, I like to compare our dreams to seeds and/or acorns.

For example, when people are on their death bed, many regret never pursuing more of their dreams. They in essence die with unplanted seeds, or pockets full of unpursued dreams. These are like seeds never planted. However, pursuing our dreams is like planting. It means we remove the seeds from our pockets and do something with them.

However, to be effective, we must first learn the best environment to plant our seeds. We need to ensure they have good soil, and the right amount of light and water. This is planning. We just don't hope something happens – that's daydreaming.

Rather, we pray about our dreams, we surrender them to God in faith, and then we become good stewards in pursuing them. We therefore plan on the best way to make them a reality. This is "planting" the seed.

Then of course, we have the work to do after the planting. We have to weed the area so that growth isn't stifled. We have to water it and tend to the garden area in general.

Likewise, with our dreams, we must not allow distractions to get us off course – these are the weeds that come. Instead, we must be committed to the task and be patient.

Eventually, the seed grows and as it matures it produces more seed. Thus, it multiplies and like an acorn, that one seed can ultimately produce a forest of new trees.

Our dreams as they mature can likewise multiply. They too can expand for a greater good and that one seed can spawn many new ones. This is the power of effective dreaming with a plan of action.

Interestingly, many of our dreams will typically require some type of financial assistance. This is where sound financial stewardship, planning, preparation, and savvy come in. They help us plant them effectively, not just haphazardly.

So, let's get started in growing our investment savvy, which plays a key role in accomplishing our various long term goals.

There are various investment theories and strategies out there, and I promise I'm not going to add another one. My goal is not to provide theories, but rather helpful insights. I'm going to share with you the strategies needed to help you better understand some of the inner-workings and basics of the investment world.

First, how do investment advisors make their money? Commissions of course, and they come in a variety of structures. You might pay transaction charges each time a stock, or investment sale and purchase is made, or you might pay an annual fee typically based on the size of your account.

For mutual funds, there are some no-load funds out there that claim not to charge any fees. However, be sure there are no maintenance, or management charges hidden somewhere. After all, the money manager and mutual fund company has to make money somehow.

Again, paying fees is not a bad thing. There is a price to doing business. Just make sure you know what you're paying. You wouldn't just walk into a car dealership and buy a car without first knowing the price would you?

In addition to knowing the fees you might pay, you can choose to venture the investment world alone, or seek a qualified advisor. A good partner is worth their weight in gold, and knowing how to pick one right for you is vital.

Investment Partner

What are some insights to keep in mind when you're interviewing advisors? Realize most firms' investment consultants are fairly similar in the beginning. Meaning they receive similar training, hold similar licenses and sell similar investment products. It's the character, tenure, and risk tolerance of each advisor that's unique and should be highly considered.

So, what training does the average investment advisor receive?

The majority of a new advisor's time is spent behind a stack of books studying. Typically, each chapter has practice exams they must pass. Then, the advisor has additional practice tests they need to pass at crash courses offered by many firms.

After weeks of intense study, taking practice exams and cramming in crash courses, the advisor prepares for their final licensing exam. Keep in mind there are several licenses they must obtain before they can begin working with clients. Each test for each license must be passed with a score of at least 70 percent. If they fail an exam, they may retake it typically two more times before a firm may decide to terminate employment. Although, many tutorials are implemented to help advisors pass their tests, some unfortunately do not. However, for those that do pass, they have another daunting task before them. They must now find clients.

The thought of newly licensed advisors offering sound investment advice may seem a bit frightening to some. After all, they lack long term investment experience and may have memorized much of the information needed to pass the tests. Even though this may be true, I'm going to share how you can best pick the best advisor for you.

Please note, I'm not saying, or suggesting you shouldn't trust, or do business with new advisors, because there are many brilliant new advisors out there. In addition, the investment firms do their best to ensure clients are managed effectively, and there are many safeguards in place to protect customers. What I am suggesting is that you get to know who you're dealing with. What is their background? How much experience do they have with investing money? My point is to ask questions and to understand the investments being proposed.

One of the goals of this book is to provide you with the knowledge that will help arm you against fraud, help you stay in control and also help you find that honest investment partner - the one that truly serves to help you steward your money.

How can you best find this partner? Again, ask questions and interview several advisors. You'll find each person you interview to be very different. Ask them for their advice on how they would invest $100k. See what they have to say. Hopefully, they will try to determine your risk tolerance and long terms plans before jumping right in on offering advice.

Also, remember to truly understand the fees involved. If your advisor doesn't know, or skips around the fee issue or simply hands you a brochure to read, take note. Make sure they know their stuff and double check their accuracy.

Another helpful tactic is to choose an advisor that puts you at ease. The one you feel most comfortable with and the one that takes the time to ask you lots of questions around your financial goals. In the end, many of the advisors may offer you similar investment options. So, be sure to compare which advisor best understands the fees charged and discloses freely how they make their money.

Understanding "The Market"

Basically, the market can be described as the

Standard and Poor's list of 500 publicly traded companies - otherwise known as the S&P 500.

The **S&P 500** includes the largest companies and represents 81 percent of the market value of all companies listed on the New York Stock Exchange.

The good news is that you can actually own this index. Interestingly, this particular index is one many money managers try to measure their funds against. Some of these managers are successful in outperforming the S&P and dominate the market short term, which is one to five years, but unfortunately, they may fail to repeat their success long term, which is ten years and longer.

In fact, some of the top performers come and go in the financial industry as fast as one-hit wonders on the Billboard Top Forty Music Count Down. Some of these funds coming and going are **blended funds**, meaning they typically own large-cap, mid-cap, or small-cap companies in various segments that can mainly be categorized as growth, or value.

Value-funds typically consist of larger companies that tend to be fairly stable and don't fluctuate in price often, or too drastically. Some examples of value companies include IBM, Johnson and Johnson and General Motors.

Growth funds can consist of larger companies, but many focus on small, or middle sized companies that tend to be in a growth mode, or in a specific industry/segment. These funds tend to be riskier and may have greater fluctuation in price than value funds.

Another division of funds are **sector** funds. What are sector funds? They are simply funds that invest in specific sectors, such as healthcare, technology, real estate, utilities and etc. These funds are riskier than blended portfolios consisting of value and/or growth companies because if a particular segment, or sector struggles so does that linking sector fund. However, the reverse is also true. If a particular sector, like healthcare, for example, does well, so does the sector fund.

A benefit and added level of security to both blended and sector funds, is the power of **diversification**. Meaning they hold a variety of companies, not just one, or two; and in the case of blended funds, they can hold various companies throughout various segments. So, if one company or sector has an off year, the hope is that other companies and segments in the fund will offset the loss.

Mutual funds are made up of stocks, but there are also funds that are made up of other funds. For example, you may have heard of **target date funds**, and this is basically what they are. This means, they allow the investor to own one mutual fund that consists of international, domestic, bond and/or other type of funds within it. Over time, the fund automatically transitions the portfolio to own less stocks and more bonds. This helps the investor in that they simply pick the "target date" they feel best represents the time they plan to retire, or will want access to the money.

In essence, the portfolio begins more aggressive and transitions to a more conservative allocation the closer one gets to the target date.

They are structured to help take a lot of the individual fund and stock picking challenges off the table for the investor and make the investment process easier.

You may have also heard of **ETFs**, or Exchange Traded Funds. These basically consist of stocks much like mutual funds do, but buy and sell, or trade, like stocks.

Ultimately, it's up to your individual risk tolerance as to which funds, and/or ETFs you prefer, if any at all.

If you plan to make a lot of individual stock trades and bond purchases you may want to consider money managers that offer fee based services and allow unlimited trades. This could save you money.

It's important to note that the size of your investment can determine certain **break points**, or discounts in the fees charged. Meaning the larger your investment, the more discounts you can potentially receive.

Again, make sure you know your consultants experience level with investments. But most importantly, do you trust them? Go with your gut instincts on this, coupled with your investigative work. If they are inexperienced, you know your risks. If you don't trust them – run!

Some other interesting insights to note that can help you maximize your investments includes buying investments for the long term.

Since its inception in 1928, the S&P 500 has had an approximate return of 8 to 10 percent.[6]

Even Warren Buffett, one of the most well-known investment experts, is known for his longer term investment strategy. One of his quotes illustrates this point further. *"In the short term the market is a popularity contest; in the long term it is a weighing machine"*.[7]

Although I do see a lot of value in buying quality investments for the long term, we want to always be sure to incorporate **rebalancing**. This is the process of periodically reviewing our portfolio to ensure we have the proper allocation of stocks, bonds, etc.

As mentioned earlier, target date funds do this automatically and an advisor will do this as well, but if you're going solo this will be up to you. Our risk tolerance can change over time and we typically don't want to be too aggressive the closer we get to retirement.

Another way to help maximize your savings is by setting up a systematic investment plan, or **SIP** to come out of your checking account monthly to make mutual fund purchases. Not only does this force you to save and benefit from market growth, but it also allows you to utilize the power of dollar-cost averaging.

Dollar cost averaging happens when you make investment purchases at different periods in time, thus allowing you to buy stocks at various price points. This allows you to benefit from the long term growth typically seen in the market. To illustrate further the power behind long term market growth, just think of inflation. Over time, most things go up in price. Remember when soda was 50 cents? Now, in many places its $1, or more!

Another advantage for holding your individual stocks and mutual funds long term is based around dividends. A **dividend** is money that companies pay out to their shareholders usually on a monthly or quarterly basis. The dividend is a powerful wealth tool if used correctly. Just imagine for a moment owning a large, respected company that annually pays $1.00 a share. Now, what if you owned 20,000 shares, or even 50,000 shares? That's $20k, or $50k a year! Not too bad – and even better, you don't have sell, or liquidate your investment. You're putting your money to work for you, long-term!

Another investment option to address is **annuities**. Annuities offer both fixed and variable rate options and allow you to benefit from tax deferred growth.

Quite simply, fixed annuities pay a fixed interest rate and offer a death benefit. Variable annuities can also offer a fixed rate, but their key feature is you can also make market investments and gain death benefits.

Annuities come with a lot of bells and whistles. So, it's important to meet with your advisor concerning your best option.

It's important to note that annuities are an insurance product and there are various fees attached to their options and supplemental benefits. In fact, entire books have been written about annuities. So, just make sure you have a clear understanding of every possible hidden and disclosed fee possible, and don't just take one person's word for it. Do your homework and take the time to interview various advisors and find the one that knows their stuff best.

While you're interviewing advisors, remember, they could also be a lending partner. There are consultants out there that can help you with all aspects of your finances. Meaning they can do investments, retail lending, and commercial lending – or they are part of a team that can assist in all these areas.

Teaming and/or positions that unify these services are a direction many firms are steering towards. Remember, one stop shopping? Now, you can work with one person, or firm on everything. And as we discussed earlier, the more you have with a particular financial institution, the more benefits you get!

Now that you know significantly more than the average person about finances and how to maximize your existing loans, deposits and investments, you have the power to develop and strengthen your finances!

Remember, it comes down to you taking the actions to create results. How will you use your new found wisdom? Will you help others? You now have the power to make changes in your financial life and for those around you.

However, before we leave finances, let's look at one last powerful money management principal - the giving plan.

GIVING PLAN

As we jump into the components of the giving plan, let me tell you about something I describe as the **70/30 Rule**. It is a basic money management practice I personally implement and practice.

Here's how it works, first, take 10 percent of your net income, after any employee retirement plan contributions, if you have one, to pay down any debts you have. This is part of your spending plan.

Second, save and invest another 10 percent as part of your savings plan.

Finally, donate the last 10 percent to your church, or charities you believe in.

You live off the remaining 70 percent of your net income.

In summary, 10 percent of income goes to savings plan, 10 percent to debt pay down as part of your spending plans, and 10 percent goes to your giving plan.

What does this look like in dollars and cents? If you have a one dollar, let's say after tax, insurance and 401k you get to take home 60 cents. From that 60 cents you give 6 cents to savings, put 6 cents on debt reduction and 6 cents given away. You keep 42 cents.

For a larger visual, let's assume you make $100k gross and keep $60k after taxes, 401k contribution and insurance, you save $6k a year, which works out to be $500 per month. This goes to help build your emergency savings, which you want to be at least enough to cover 3 to 6 months in living expenses. This also helps build your vacation, wedding, and other saving goals.

The other $500 per month goes to help expedite your debt reduction and the last $500 per month to charitable giving. You live off the remaining $42k, or $3500 per month.

Now, I realize this may seem crazy to some. You might be thinking you're lucky to live on what you have, but if you practice this formula, it can help to greatly reduce financial worries. For your debts will be going down, your savings will be going up, and your giving will be making impact!

I'm sure, you've also heard at some time in your life the importance and value of saving, paying down debt, and giving. Now, implement this practice and make it a habit. I'm not saying it will be easy at first – it most likely won't be, but neither is starting a healthy diet, exercise routine, or anything else that's constructive. These things are never easy – but you and future generations will be glad you made the sacrifice.

Now, why should we have a giving plan? Well, we are told that living generously is good for us in several passages of Scripture. Such as "it is more blessed to give" in Acts 20:35 and "whoever sows bountifully will also reap bountifully" in 2 Corinthians 9:6, just to name a few.

We are also told a cheerful giver is loved by God in 2 Corinthians 9:7. Clearly, we see giving is important to God and of course we know God is generous, therefore, so should His children be.

But if this still isn't enough reason, there are proven health benefits shared throughout various media resources - these include an increase in our sense of gratitude, happiness, stress reduction, and even lower blood pressure.

Still need convincing? Generosity helps contribute to a greater good. Hoarding helps no one, not even the hoarder, but giving helps the giver and others -

all while pleasing God. Therefore, it's wise to have a giving plan, because when we budget a certain amount to give and then seek ways to give, we are more likely to do it and reap the benefits.

I would consider myself a generous person, but I don't think it's a natural gift of mine. I have to work at it – make an effort at it. Instead, my impulse is to save more and spend more because this directly benefits me and my family. Many of us can fall into this mindset, which is why establishing an intentional giving plan is so beneficial.

However, there are others who truly possess a natural inclination to giving. My wife is one of these people. In fact, I jokingly ask her to not give away our house – just yet. I honestly think she could. She is one of those who give naturally, abundantly, and enthusiastically. I truly admire her in this area. Thankfully, I have discovered a secret that allows me to share in her giving spirit.

Early in our marriage, I would often stifle her giving. I would encourage her not to give so much, but to rather consider our needs. This of course has some truth in it, but would only result in diluting her joy and creating conflict in our marriage.

I was focused on our saving and spending, as she was, but she was also focusing on giving, when I wasn't. In time, I acknowledged the fact that I may never be as generous as her, but I could participate by not silencing hers.

As a result, my giving gets to piggy-back off hers. So, as a married couple, our giving is multiplied.

This may be helpful to others who aren't as naturally giving as others.

We can establish a process to give, which is good, but we can also support others in their generosity rather than stifle it. By supporting it, we participate in their gifting, which in time unifies our ability to make impact.

Today, my wife and I have very few disagreements about money, like we used to. She knows our budget. I include her in on what we save, what we spend, and what we give, and I am included on what she spends and gives. She trusts me in the savings category – like I trust her in the giving one.

Heart Of The Matter

As mentioned, I wasn't and haven't always been a cheerful giver. In fact, I recall the first conviction I had to begin tithing. I knew the 10 percent axiom, but I went back and forth on this with God for a while. I researched commentary and Biblical references on the subject of tithing and practically tried every way possible to cleanse my conscience of the conviction to give. Again, this is embarrassing to admit today, but it's true.

God says He wants a cheerful giver and to give the amount we have decided in our heart. This frees up the 10 percent question, but raises another one. As a pastor once said, "Why would any believer living under God's grace do less than a believer did under the law"? So, why would we not do at least 10 and more?

I had to consider - if I truly trusted God to meet all my needs, I wouldn't hesitate to adhere to His promptings to give. Ultimately, the reason I hesitated was because I didn't trust Him fully.

So, I started with giving on my net. For the Bible also says to give on your increase. So, my "actual" increase, as I justified it, was the amount my bank account "increased".

Also, I was joyful in this process. I gave 10 percent off my net for many years, and I had some very prosperous years. I didn't back down when I received six figure bonus checks either. I eagerly gave God 10 percent of any increase I ever received.

Then, one day I felt convicted to give off my gross. So, I tried this, but I was grumpy! My joy transferred to grumbling. My joy of giving was being diluted and as I prayed over this, I felt God say to me, "I don't need your money, Dagan. I want your heart. Don't bother giving if you can't be happy about it."

So, I thanked God and went back to giving on my net increase and my joy returned.

Then, after some time, the conviction to give on gross came back, but this time I had a different response, because my faith had matured. I knew God wasn't after "my money." For it's all His anyway. He's working on my heart, and now He was revisiting because I had become "comfortable" in my giving.

I have heard God likes to convict the comfortable and comfort the convicted, or something like that. However the saying goes, I get the point and tend to agree.

Whenever I come to a comfort point in my walk with Christ, something seems to get stirred up. Why? I believe, because He desires growth and maturity and as soon as we get comfortable, it's time to start growing again.

Thus, the point to my giving. He knew I was willing, but my heart wasn't quite there yet. So, He gave it time and came back. This time I did something I would have never thought to do before. My budget would get all out of balance if I started giving more, but then something occurred to me. What if I made some cuts to my savings plan? If I cut back there, I could invest more in my giving plan!

I actually couldn't believe the idea myself. Cut back on the amount I was saving in order to give more?

You see, when I first tried to give on my gross, I wasn't willing to make any cuts. I wasn't about to cut my savings, but this time, in order to increase my giving, I was willing to make some personal sacrifice.

I still can't believe it, but I rejoice! Interestingly enough, I can now give on my gross and do it joyfully! I trust He can make up the difference in my savings plan if He chooses to. Although, even with the cut-back, I'm still saving over the 10 percent described in the 70/30 plan.

We must understand that God isn't interested in our money – He's interested in our hearts, and often times He uses money to accomplish this task.

I have heard the word testimony is just another way to say, "test-of-money." How true this is for me. God has used money to break me and grow me in so many ways, and I believe He does the same with countless others.

Money is not the root of evil. The love of it is. So, God often uses money in various ways to break us of our love for it in order to refocus our devotions to Him. He wants our dependency and security to be based on Him – not our bank accounts.

In the end, the argument to the tithing on net and gross doesn't need to get legalistic. It's a heart thing. And I firmly believe, the more we follow Him, and the more our love for Him grows, and our faith matures, our giving can't help but follow. It will grow too – it can't do otherwise. For God is a cheerful and gracious giver, and He desires His blessings to us to flow through us to others.

Stagnation in our giving limits our growth as believers. Jonah 2:8 is a powerful verse that touches on this point when it says, "those who cling to worthless idols turn away from God's love for them".

The ultimate question for me was and is, "what worthless things do I try to cling to." When I'm honest with myself, I was clinging to my savings account. I was clinging to building my nest egg more than being willing to submit to the conviction to give more.

This breaks my heart, but I am thankful for this realization. For God opened my eyes to see where my heart was. So, to cut back on savings to give more may seem foolish to some, but that's nothing new for those who follow Christ.

For His ways seem foolish to the world.

Do we give on gross, or net is not the question – the question is to what is our heart clinging? And for many, what we cling to may be routine struggle of surrender. The key is acknowledging it, recognizing it, and returning to our true Source of security.

In closing, and as we know, couples can quickly discover difficulty when their money habits are not aligned. For one may spend too much, keep secret money stashes, have a tendency to hoard, and others may not give at all. This dynamic only creates conflict.

The key is to communicate about money. Get on the same page, establish a process like the 70/30 plan and support one another with implementing it.

Financial literacy is an area of stewardship that doesn't develop on its own. Good money management requires sacrifice, work, and intent. However, as mentioned, our perspective of money and its prioritization in our life directly propels our ability to establish truly effective financial plans.

Money is a great tool, but a terrible master. The world tends to respect and admire those rich in material success, but true peace and fulfillment can never come from just money. Thus, money is not the ultimate goal.

Being a better steward is part of it, but maturing in our perspective is vital. Money can never be the "carrot" that leads us. It can never be the thing that guides us and dictates our choices. However, as we know, this is often the case. As a result, many families suffer, health suffers and faith stagnates, as money takes the lead.

Therefore, let us move to the other area essential to prosperous stewardship - family. This is one I nearly destroyed - completely unknowingly and innocently, but thankfully, if there's hope for me, there's hope for many more.

II

FAMILY

"What can you do to promote world peace? Go home and love your family".[9]

- Mother Teresa

Family is clearly a vital piece in promoting a fulfilled life. Without a strong family, it is more difficult to maximize all our stewardship opportunities due to potential distractions and added financial burdens.

The Bible says it best when it states that "two are better than one, because they have a good return for their work. If one falls down, he can be helped up. But pity the man who falls and has no one to help him up!" (Ecclesiastes 4:9).

I have experienced in my life the true value of family, and this is part of my testimony. It is an area many take for granted until it's gone. Sadly, many simply learn to survive with a weak family foundation, or they live with deep regrets the rest of their life.

However, success in this area means you have a

strong support system to help lift you up when life gets difficult. It means you have a safe place to come home to. Not a perfect home, but one filled for the most part with love, joy, compassion, and laughter. Who doesn't desire that?

What if you're single? Well, family still applies. None of us can escape our family and if family members aren't around, instinct typically drives us to create one. Thus, we tend to find a partner somewhere and generate a close group of friends naturally. People, even the most isolating and introverted need other people.

Surrounding yourself with the wrong people, rather than positive influences can have grave effects on our ultimate success. In fact, who you surround yourself with can limit success, or propel it.

When you self-reflect, is your family a source of motivation and empowerment, or is it a source of stress, sorrow, and frustration?

No matter which it is, have you considered how it got that way? How did it become a source of positive or negative emotion? Was it always that way?

The first step to making family more solid and strong is to understand and dissect its status today. Identify where it was, where it is, and how the current situation evolved. How did we get to where we are, and how do we get to where we want to go?

Again, if you're single – what is the family you have built for yourself? Is it a source of positive, or negative emotion?

When you can see where you are, you can then begin to take the steps necessary to make it what you want it to be.

For me personally, I am married to my college sweetheart and have two loving children. They provide me with tremendous love and joy and we depend on each other daily. We work to make the time to have sit-down dinners together. We work to have bedtime stories. We work to attend every sporting practice and game we can. We work to spend many of our weekends together. Quite simply, we work hard to do the best we can to ensure we have quality time as a family. It's not perfect, but we try.

However, as I mentioned, and if you were to ask my

wife, she would admit our family wasn't, and I wasn't always this way. Nor, did I try so hard. In fact, she would say after our first child was born, I was somewhat detached. Now, it's hard to admit, but she's right. I wasn't always as involved and committed to spending quality time together, but I have worked to change and get better every day.

Like many people, I was too busy thinking about work when I was at home. I was thinking about how I was going to hit my annual quota, or goal. I was worried about whether or not a sales contract was going to close on time. I was worried about making enough money to support my family, but in the meantime, I was missing the point. I was too busy running from a childhood of poverty and chasing a dream I had of wealth.

I was blinded by ambition - but it was the wrong ambition. For if I had gained all the money in the world and lost my family in the process, I would have nothing. In addition, I realized that I was spending much of my spare time worrying. So, when I was with my child, my body was there, but my mind was somewhere else.

Have you ever caught yourself in this situation? It's hard not to get this way quite honestly. We have so many commitments and stressors in our life that sitting and playing with blocks can be quite difficult at times. We have bills to pay, deals to make, chores to do, and a house to keep up. The list of things to do is endless and unfortunately, sometimes the ones we love and need the most get our second best. But we can resolve it in our minds to feel less guilty by telling ourselves we're doing all we do to ensure a better life for them.

We work endlessly to make the money to provide our family with the things we think they need. When all they really need is our time. A song, popular many years ago, *Cat's In The Cradle* by Harry Chapin, describes this very situation. It's about a father that worked all the time and had little time to play with his son, but his son idolized his father and said he was going to be just like him some day. Well, some day comes and the father as an old man begins to seek that time lost with his son, but now, the son doesn't have time for him. In essence, he became just like his father.

This is a sad story, but so true for many of us. The good news is that it's really never too late to change. We can retrain the way we look at priorities. We can redefine our definition of what success is, and we can redefine wealth.

So, how do we stop worrying about paying the bills, fixing the house, making more money, and all the other distractions we deal with daily to truly focus on those who matter most? Well, we do it by realizing our family's importance. After all, our family is our legacy. They are what we leave behind after we're gone.

This isn't easy stuff, yet it's very simple. The challenge is reconditioning our old habits, creating new ones, and refocusing our priorities. What's most important in life? Is it work? Is it our house, or what car we drive? Will any of that matter when we're dead? How do we want to be remembered? What do we want people to say about us if we were to die tomorrow? I know this sounds morbid, but it's true. My wife hates it when I tell her that I think about getting in a deadly car crash some mornings, simply to remind myself to not rush out the door so quickly. Instead, give a few more kisses. Hear a few more of my kids' stories, and steal a few more hugs from my wife.

This helps me slow down. I think about what if I was to die today and it reminds me of what matters. It's not the office. I wouldn't think a second about it if I was being lifted out of a car wreck on a life flight. I would be thinking about my wife and my kids - my family. Do they know how much I love them? Did I tell them enough? Did I hug and kiss them enough? Did I spend as much quality time as I could with them? Did I teach them valuable lessons that will help them be contributors to society and not takers? Did I love enough?

Not to ramble, but these are questions I don't want in my mind. In fact, I want to know full heartedly, I've done all I can. I want to leave with confidence and peace in my soul. No doubts.

So, again, it may be seen as morbid, but it works for me. It helps slow me down and set my priorities straight. The bottom line is I've changed. My wife can tell you I'm not the same father and husband. Not that I was terrible. I wasn't, but now I work to be there more, not just physically, but mentally and spiritually.

I know many of you can relate to what I'm saying. It's when your mind wanders off to other things and you become distracted when you're trying to spend that special time with your family. It's hard, but remember what do you want your legacy to be?

WORK-LIFE BALANCE

We hear the phrase, work life balance so often, and wonder if we can really have it. Some of us can say yes and some of us no, but I know we all want more of it. Interestingly, work, as indicated in the Bible, is a blessing (Ecclesiastes 5:18-19). In fact, we should rejoice in our labor for it is a gift from God.

So, if work is a gift, then why do we let it become a burden? After all, family and love is also a gift that must be nurtured. The answer is quite simple, although not very romantic – poor scheduling. If you have a smartphone, or some type of organizer then don't forget to schedule home time. Make that as important as any meeting, or conference call you may have. Again, schedule it and keep it.

I mentioned that I have had the opportunity to meet, work with, and learn from some of the most successful people in various industries, and one question I enjoyed asking them was is work life balance possible? Can one truly be successful in their career, be financially secure, and have a strong, loving family life at the same time? The answer has been yes 90 percent of the time, but they all stated the family must be made a priority - some had obviously learned this the hard way.

Soccer games, dinners, school functions, breakfast, whatever it is, schedule it and keep it, just as if it were a can't miss meeting at work. Again, maybe this isn't the most romantic, but it works.

Now, the trick is that once you have a family event scheduled - keep it. We must now be there in not just body, but in mind and spirit. That's the hardest part for those attached to their cell phone like me. This can be painful, but just think, what do you do when you're in a client meeting? You have voice mail, right? You return your calls and emails after you finish your meeting? So, we need to do the same with our family events. Let voice mail get it. Don't be at a soccer game, or at the breakfast table on the phone. Return the call – you do it at work and in businesses meetings. So let's do it when we're with our family too. We always have time to return messages, but we may not always have another opportunity to impact one of the most crucial elements in our life – family.

Obviously, there are emergency situations and exceptions that will require our immediate attention no matter where we are, but for the most part, if we work on not being distracted from family functions, we can reduce life's stresses.

Just recently I had another reminder how easy it is for me to slip back into old patterns. Remember, I am a workaholic in "recovery." So, this is an ongoing process for me. For example, just the other day as I was putting my son to bed, he said something to me that broke my heart, but was a welcome wake-up call for me to get back on track.

As I was tucking him in, he said, "Dad – sometimes I feel like I get on your nerves, when I come up to you and you're in the middle of something."

I assume we have all had these moments when our kids come up to us and we are in fact in the middle of something, but it's not earth shattering stuff. It's the stuff that can actually wait. Perhaps we're reading an article online, or looking for something. We're in the middle of something for sure, and even though we could take a break for a moment, the interruption is still unwelcome.

Perhaps this is just me. Maybe I'm the only one who acts agitated when interrupted from something "unimportant", but I admit it.

As I confessed earlier, I know I can be selfish, as most people can, and even though God has gotten my attention, I still have bouts with it and He sends these gentle and loving reminders to get my attention.

I naturally told my son he doesn't get on my nerves, and I quickly apologized for giving him that impression. I confessed to him sometimes I get focused on something and may act like that, but that he is always welcome to come to me.

That's all he needed to hear. We hugged, said we loved each other, and he went to bed peacefully knowing daddy loves him.

Can our kids and even our spouses get on our nerves at times – sure. That's normal, but I'm thankful he's secure enough to come to me about it. I'm also thankful God opened my blinders enough to acknowledge I can get a little too intense at times.

This was a subtle, but profound healing moment for us both and a perfect example that the balancing act is more like a rebalancing process. Just like the tires on our car will get out of balance periodically – we can expect the same to be true for ourselves. Thankfully, we can quickly get rebalanced and back on track.

Family Bonds

Now that we discovered some ways to help us juggle the work life balance challenge, does it also apply to extended family? Does this mean we need to spend time with our in-laws and for that matter our own mothers and fathers? Well, I leave that up to you. I don't know your past experiences with your parents, in-laws, grandparents, aunts and uncles, but for me, I know this still remains my weakest area. I'm working on my immediate family, as mentioned, which I define as my wife and kids, but too often, I can go days, or weeks not talking to my own father, mother, or sister - and we all live in the same town.

This can happen easily because we get busy with work, tending to our immediate family, and scraping for enough spare time to achieve some personal goals. When do we have time for all these other people?

One person I desire to have a closer relationship with is my father. To give you some idea why, my parents divorced when I was young and my father was in the military. He traveled across the world often and was not physically present most of my adolescent days, not by any neglect of his own. He quite simply was in Korea, Germany, or some other station and couldn't be at many events. So, with physical distance, emotional distance is often a result. This is the case with my father, but now, he is retired and lives thirty minutes away.

Now is the opportunity to catch up on lost time, but to be honest, I'm so used to him not being available, my habits cause me to forget he's so close. It's quite innocent. I'm simply not used to him being so nearby. I forget and get caught up with other things.

So, as with other important scheduled events, we're trying to schedule more things together. It's not perfect, but it's getting better.

I also work to schedule lunches with my mother, and others I care about – not perfect, but trying.

Again, some of you may think this is very impersonal, scheduling time with your parents like it's something to strike off a to-do list. Well, to be honest, it is. It is something I consider important enough to write down and ensure gets done.

That's all a to-do list is anyway. Things we don't, or can't forget to do. Things so important we take the time to write them down and make sure they are completed.

Naturally, I don't know your situation, but I can suggest that if you desire to stay in better touch with loved ones and friends, and know you're doing a poor job with it now, and you realize your family is not as strong as it can be - then do something about it. Do something beginning today and you will find your life more fulfilled, less stressed, and you will come closer to realizing redefined wealth.

I realize families come in all varieties. You may be divorced and your kids live far away, like my situation was. Or, there may be other obstacles in your way. Here's some insight that may help. Think about if that person were in trouble and needed you. Perhaps they were in an accident, what would you do to make sure you saw them?

Would you find the time? Would you find the money? Would you do whatever you had to do to be there with them? Of course you would. Well with any goal, the only way we achieve them is by having a strong enough desire to do so. For example, someone once said if you can't list at least 7 reasons why you want something then it's not something you really want. The goal doesn't have a strong enough validation. It's simply something that would be nice to have, but it doesn't pull you.

The subject of family however reaches beyond those who simply share the same blood with us. Meaning, if we are Christians, our family also includes the family of believers. God says is Psalm 68:6 that He sets the lonely in families.

This is a beautiful picture and one of great hope. For I realize some are without any family. Some come from extremely broken homes. However, for believers, we are a part of God's family through our faith is Jesus Christ.

In the book of John, verses 19:26-27, a vivid picture to the expanded view of family is highlighted. Jesus is dying on the cross, and He looks down to His friend John and entrusts the care of His mother, Mary, to him. It's interesting He doesn't look to His brothers to do this. Jesus did have brothers, but He entrusts His mother's care to His friend, John.

In the body of Christ, family is expanded. Family is about faith. Family gets a new identity. We see this with adoption. Nonblood members, become family.

Likewise, we are adopted into God's family and

immediately get new family members.

So, do we spend time with them as well? This is what makes fellowship so special. We come to church each week for a family reunion to celebrate our Father. We praise Him, pray to Him, and learn more about Him at a weekly family reunion.

One thing we can all do as believers is to never neglect this coming together. Church isn't the building – it's the people of God coming together. Setting all else aside and prioritizing Him above all, and doing it with family.

RESPONSIBILITIES & ROLES

Another powerful tool, or better yet, perspective I have gained since surrendering my life to Christ is understanding His role in my life and as a result, my role in my immediate family's life.

Clearly, for believers Jesus is both our Lord and Savior. This means He saves us from sin, gives us eternal life and serves as the Boss, or the King over every aspect of our life.

However, within these roles, He accomplishes much more. He is also our **Pastor**, our **Protector**, our **Provider,** and equips and prepares us for what He calls us to in life. In turn, I realized, I am to do the same in my family's life. For we are reflections of Christ.

Therefore, we are to be the pastor of our family. We may have church pastors, but they are there to help and come along side us. It is our job and responsibility to be the primary pastor of our home. This means we must know our Bible, study the Word of God, be the first to attend worship, to take notes, and to take this role seriously in order to teach and role model this in our families. 1 Peter 5:2 provides a beautiful illustration of this as it encourages us to eagerly care for the flock God has entrusted to us.

Interestingly, ever since I began taking this pastor role seriously, God has put me to work. For example, it wasn't long after He led me to teach an adult Bible study class at church, which resulted in me being invited to be a deacon, which led to me going on a mission trip to Africa, which led to a second trip to Africa with my youngest son, which led to serving on church committees. All because I started getting serious about Jesus, He began getting serious about putting me to work - and I love it!

It wasn't until I was 40 years old that I saw a grown man pray voluntarily. I have seen people pray of course, but it wasn't until I went on my first mission trip to Africa that I witnessed a fully grown man, get out of bed, rub the sleep from his eyes and head straight to his Bible. I caught this man doing this and then praying quietly on the patio - all by himself, and all on his own accord, because he wanted to.

Now, I had been doing this myself for nearly a decade, but seeing another man had a great impact. It was then I realized the importance of my children seeing me pray – voluntarily.

Thankfully, my children have grown up "catching" me praying. Ever since they were little, they would walk in on me while I was on my hands and knees praying.

But it wasn't until I saw another man doing this did I realize the impact.

I thanked God for the grace He gave me. I am so thankful that despite all my mistakes, all my imperfections, and all my faults that my children have always seen me pray. For this wasn't always the case, as I've mentioned, but to them, this is what they have always seen – thankfully.

The lesson – let others catch us in the act of praying. Not because it's an act we perform in order to be seen, but because it's a habit we do.

Our other role is that of protector and it goes far beyond ensuring we have a home security system. Rather, it is all about protecting our loved ones the best we can from the seductions and evils of this world. Psalm 82:4 tells us to rescue the weak and needy and to deliver them from the hand of the wicked.

This, to me, doesn't mean we keep our families in a bubble, but it does mean we teach them to the dangers and temptations of life. How to guard themselves spiritually, emotionally and physically. It means we don't allow certain television shows, songs, internet sites, etc. in our house. It means we do whatever we can to keep from putting stumbling blocks in their life and to replace them with stepping stones.

For me, I deleted certain songs from my playlist, but the biggest move I made was alcohol. I removed it from my life. Let me first say I'm not pointing a finger at Christians who drink. I am simply saying it was a potential stumbling block in my life that had to go. I don't miss it now, but at first, I never thought I could have pizza without a beer.

However, it ultimately became an easy thing to give up, because I was convicted to do so in my role as their protector. The only point here is do whatever is necessary to serve as protector. Sacrifice what you must. For that is what a protector does.

Our other role is that of provider. Philippians 2:4 encourages us to look out for the interests of others, as well as our own.

Clearly, we can trick ourselves into thinking this is limited to monetary provisions, but of course, it goes far beyond anything money can provide. We need to provide for the spiritual and emotional aspects of our family as well.

This means we invest time with them. One way I try to do this is having Daddy Dates with my kids. I will take my daughter out on a date, and I will take my son out as well. Just the two of us. We spend this time talking about the things going on in their life, and what's important to them.

I want to learn more about them and get to know

their hearts and dreams. I also share what's going on with me so that they can get to know my heart and dreams. Malachi 4:6 says that God will turn the hearts of the parents to their children and the hearts of the children to their parents – I desire this.

Then of course, my wife and I set time together to catch up and to share moments, make memories, and kindle the fires so that they remain ablaze for years to come.

The other two roles are that of prayer and preparer. Clearly, we must serve as the prayer warrior for our families - to pray together as a family, to lead those prayers, and to make our alone time with God a primary priority. I love starting my day with Bible study and prayer in the early hours of the morning. I seek His guidance, direction and it just gets my day off to the right start. We then end our day as a family, praying together before bed. Then of course, I find time to pray with my kids and my wife separately periodically throughout the week. The point is we are intentional and consistent with prayer and it is an integral part of our life.

This helps me also better prepare and teach all the things God desires me to pass on - like my faith. But also, how to steward and manage their money, and other areas of life. When we consider it, we have quite a privilege and opportunity to help prepare others in this life as purveyors of hope and encouragement!

This mirrors the Chinese proverb that says, "Give a man a fish and you feed him for a day. Teach him to fish, and you feed him for a lifetime".

As we conclude the topic of family, now is a good time to review and refresh your goals. Write them all and beside each one in a separate column, identify at least 7 reasons why you desire to accomplish that particular goal. If you can't, scratch that goal off. Now, review which goals are left. These are the goals you have passion for. You may want to even write them down in a prayer journal to keep track of them, and pray over routinely. For these are things you truly desire. All that's left is to take action. Remember, baby steps.

We're now ready to discover insights concerning our health. This stewardship area is often neglected, or idolized. However, there is some good news!

III

FITNESS

"The first wealth is health."[10]

- Ralph Waldo Emerson

We're redefining wealth and the way we look at riches. For a moment, think about some of the people you know with money. How is their physical health? For that matter, how is yours?

I know countless people in terrible shape physically, and I know others that care for their bodies as vigorously as possible. For they realize it fuels their energy and mental aptitude to keep going and to conquer even more aspirations.

I've experienced the consequences of living too fast and neglecting my body. I say fortunately, because I personally know the benefits and pitfalls our actions can have on health. We cannot even begin to fully accomplish all we can achieve in life if we do not have the proper energy, and we will not be able to completely enjoy the fruits of our labor until we have the proper health to do so.

Good health and energy is essential to accomplishing our goals. Good health prospers a quick mind. It maintains our momentum to complete our journey.

For example, let's assume you own a Ferrari convertible. Are you going to fill it up with diesel when it calls for the highest octane of unleaded? Of course not! You're going to make sure nothing but premium gasoline goes in. After all, you made a major investment in the car and you want to keep it running smooth. You most likely keep it polished and clean too! I bet you keep it in a garage rather than outside as well. And you probably are extremely careful not to scratch it. My point is you take extra care of your investment. Well, what greater asset do we have than our bodies? The human body is the one of the most miraculous things ever created. It's absolutely a miraculous creation and quite beautiful.

If you think about how much our bodies do, how magnificent our minds are and how powerful our will to live is, it's shameful to think how much we neglect it. Unlike the luxury car, a piece of metal, we may put "low octane fuel" into our systems. In fact, we're quite careless and don't do half the things we should to keep this wonderful creation running well. We often keep it running at low gear, and rarely give it the opportunity to show us what it can really do. Just think of all the things you've accomplished in your life with your mind and body despite the neglect it's received and imagine what you could do with maximized energy.

Even the Bible tells us that our body is not our own, but was bought at a price and is owned by God (1 Corinthians 6:19-20). So, if we believe this to be true, why wouldn't we take the better care of ourselves?

WE ARE WHAT WE EAT

I know I was running at half steam for far too many years. I used to pick up a sausage biscuit for breakfast, eat pizza, fried wings, or hamburgers for lunch and a steak for dinner, or some other meat. Then I would toss it all back with beer and/or wine. On top of that, I used to smoke on occasions and eventually moved to smokeless tobacco. Today, I can't imagine how I got anything done, but I did and did quite well despite myself. Unfortunately, it was taking a toll on my body. A toll I couldn't physically see.

I was overweight for my height, but didn't appear to be in bad health. However, I didn't realize what was truly going on inside my body. Then I decided to get some life insurance and had to have blood work done. That's when the true story was revealed and it wasn't good. To give you an idea, most medical doctors don't want your triglyceride level, which is basically a measure of the fat in your blood, to exceed 200. Mine was over 980! Basically, my body was in distress before I was even thirty years old. In fact, one doctor told me I was at risk to have a stroke and/or heart attack before I reached forty if I continued on the same path.

I had a choice to make and it was not easy. How could it be easy? I love food. I knew I had to change my eating habits and give up all that good stuff. I had to start exercising more too. Although I used to be a strong rower, swimmer and runner, I had gotten out of the habit and trying to get back in the habit was going to be tough, and I knew it. But I had more than 7 reasons as to why I wanted to achieve my goal. Mainly, my wife and kids, and I definitely didn't want a heart attack. My grandmother had two open heart procedures, and I realized my chances for the same were increasing.

In life, we only have two decisions to make - constructive, or destructive. I decided to take action and make a constructive one.

First, I simply tried to exercise more and continue to eat mostly what I wanted, but that didn't work well enough. It was tough in the beginning to even find the time to jog at least twenty minutes three days a week, but I kept at it and eventually worked my way up thirty minutes four days a week. However, it still wasn't enough. Blood work still indicated higher triglyceride levels than preferred by doctors.

By now, many would start taking medicine and for good reason, but my wife and I decided to try and treat it with diet and exercise first.

So, the next step was diet. I cut out most meats because of the saturated fat content, but I continued to eat fish, just no pork, chicken, or red meat. This helped a little more, but I still wasn't down to where I needed to be. Frustrated and angry, I felt defeated. I was angry at my body for being cursed with bad cholesterol. Why me? I have friends who can eat whatever they want and their blood levels are just fine. How did I get so unlucky?

After my pity party, I sought more advice from heart specialists. My wife being a nurse knew about some books that taught about "healing" foods. Basically, foods that help our bodies, rather than hurt them.

By simply avoiding some foods and eating more of the "good" foods, studies show a person can add years to their life, help heal their bodies, and increase resistance to various diseases.[8]

By adapting to this new way of eating, I began feeling better than I ever had! For example, I had more energy and my thinking was clearer. I didn't feel so sluggish, or get tired after eating. Instead, I felt energized and weight literally began dropping off!

Starting out, I worked to avoid enriched white flour, meat other than fish, and foods high in sugar, including alcohol.

What did this leave me with to eat and drink? Mainly organic fruits, vegetables, nuts, beans and whole grains, soy or almond milk and water. Not much of the old food I used to eat, but then again, it wasn't helping me, and this food was.

Am I advocating that to achieve health success that we have to give up meat? Absolutely not! It's what I needed to do for my health. You may not have the same problems I have. You most likely have different ones. What I am suggesting though is that you identify your problems and fix them.

Do you need to lose weight? Do you eat a lot of unhealthy food? Do you know what is healthy and what is not? Most of us think we know what's bad for us and what's good for us. I think most of us also know there is good fat and bad fat, but do you know which foods to consume the most of and which ones to avoid and/or keep in moderation? I didn't.

Basically, I learned to eat primarily green leafy vegetables, hard vegetables, fruits and beans. Some examples include foods such as spinach and romaine lettuce, which are both very high in protein, calcium and iron. I also learned that when eating nuts it's important to eat them raw, not roasted and salted. They maintain more of their nutrition that way.

I also had to learn to keep my meat and dairy intake at a minimum – which hasn't been easy and to eat organic produce whenever possible.

Dagan J. Sharpe

In addition, and as stated earlier, I try to stay clear from those refined grains, including white flour. Unfortunately, this is a lot of the tasty stuff, including donuts, pizza, biscuits, and etc. This continues to be one of my hardest habits to break, because I love carbs!

To clarify, I went very strict in the beginning. Now, after years of better eating, exercising and sleeping habits, I allow myself to indulge a little more in foods I truly enjoy, but I still keep it reigned in from what it once was.

Other benefits to changing my eating habits in addition to the wait-loss, is higher energy levels and an increased tolerance to sickness. In fact, I can't recall the last time I had a cold and this is living in a house with two kids.

How does my diet help increase my tolerance? Since I eat mostly fruits, vegetables, beans and nuts, I take in more antioxidants, vitamins and nutrients than I used to. For example, studies show that foods like blueberries contain high levels of antioxidants which help strengthen immune systems, and some peppers contain more vitamin C than an orange! Better yet, this is just the tip of the iceberg. The list of healing foods truly goes on and on. To learn more, I recommend reading some books written by medical doctors and nutritionists so that you can benefit from their in depth knowledge. I'm one of their "book" patients and thankful for it.

So, can you change your eating habits, exercise more, get adequate sleep, build a stronger body, and most importantly, pursue better health? You can, but it is hard work – at least for me, but I have the desire to accomplish this goal. What are your 7 reasons?

THE POWER OF EXERCISE

We have all heard the power behind exercise. It releases endorphins which enhance our stamina, sex drive, and overall mood. We become more positive, and feel more attractive. In addition, our confidence explodes. Even better is your motivation will pick up as you begin to see the new you emerge. Your clothes will fit looser, your skin will look younger, and your eyes sparkle. You won't feel sluggish or tired as often and you won't need so many pick me ups, such as coffee, or slow me downs, such as alcohol.

If you don't exercise, start by walking at least

twenty minutes a day and work your way up. All you have to do is give up one television program. Some of us spend hours watching TV, when we could be doing something productive to better ourselves and accomplish our goals. Spend thirty minutes walking instead of watching TV and replace your bad snack food with good snack food, such as organic raisins.

I admit my exercise routine was hard to start, but now it's hard to stop. I find that I have to go running. My body compels me to not miss a scheduled day and if I do, I have to make it up, not by choice, but by desire. I truly need my exercise. My body craves it, and I feel better for it.

Sound good? Then start your exercise routine today! Don't wait. Go walking and work your way up to jogging, if not running, try biking, if not biking, swimming, if not swimming, find something to keep your heart rate up over thirty minutes. Your efforts will be greatly rewarded and best of all, you get to see the results and realize a new, more energized life.

Just think for a moment if you didn't have your health, but had success in your finances, spirituality and family. What would be missing? The answer is a lot. If you were sick or tired all the time, you wouldn't be able to enjoy your family to the fullest, or give them your undivided attention.

If you had poor health propelled by lifestyle choices, you may be limited in enjoying some of the benefits money provides, such as going on active vacations and devoting the energy needed to the interests and hobbies you enjoy most. Perhaps you couldn't serve as many people as you wanted to, or give all that you truly wanted to give.

As I began my new eating and exercise lifestyle, I was surprised to find how many people were doing the same thing. For example, I once thought vegetarians were radical. It's just an image I had. That's not to mention what I thought about vegans, who don't eat, or consume any animal products. I really thought they were radical, but the more I live the lifestyle, the more I realize there are many just like me - people simply trying to live a healthier lifestyle. Some may have varying reasons, but many eat organic fruits and vegetables, nuts and beans as a primary diet because it helps them feel better and improve their health.

In fact, the organic produce industry is experiencing record breaking sales and new grocery stores catering to this preference are expanding and even popular main stream grocers are stocking more organic and vegetarian produce. Again, it's catching on, but I want you to know I'm not against eating meat. In truth, I love juicy porterhouse steaks, thick hamburgers, bacon, sausage and everything else that's meat. It was just not processing well with my body, and I had to make a change – a course correction.

I may cheat on my diet now and again, but for the most part, my eating habits are permanent, and I am living stronger and healthier for it.

Remember, the steps to creating "abundant supplies" are easy. It's the action and actual implementation of the steps that is difficult. So, to help strengthen and empower your health goals, list your 7 reasons for accomplishing them.

I hope your definition of wealth is changing as we progress through each chapter. Our next topic is the most personal of all. It is more intimate and more powerful than all the others combined. It's the most dynamic because success here is constantly growing and expanding. It is the most powerful, because it is the driving force behind the completion of any desired goal.

I am excited, honored, and humbled to share the insights I have gained regarding faith – for some came the hard way. However, no matter where you are in your spiritual journey, if you desire to grow more, that's the perspective from which we begin.

Dagan J. Sharpe

FULL DISCLOSURE

IV

FAITH

"Faith is taking the first step even when you don't see the whole staircase".[11]

- Martin Luther King, Jr.

Welcome to the most profound and challenging stewardship area of all. Why? Because so many of us struggle to devote the time needed to succeed in it. It should be our center, our focus. If it is, all things work out for our ultimate good and benefit (Romans 8:28).

And I'm not talking about a prosperity gospel – that's not biblical. Rather, pain, hardship, brokenness, and trials are a part of life and there is no formula to escape from them. Nor should there be.

A wonderful example of this is the Japanese art known as Kintsugi. This is where broken pottery is repaired with an adhesive mixed with gold. The result is a new work of art made more beautiful than the original.

Likewise, in Christ, our brokenness is made beautiful. For what is broken mends stronger.

This is a truth that took me awhile to understand, but it wasn't until I was broken – broken of my pride, arrogance, selfishness, ego, vanity, and greed was God able to begin His healing. Then, through faith, He began to use my broken areas as a ministry, and build my testimony.

However, this just doesn't happen. We play a part. Yet, so many believers seem to hit a growth stall after salvation – but there's so much more!

We are saved through our faith in Jesus Christ (John 3:16). Testifying that He is God in the flesh, who came to earth to be crucified, buried, and raised to give all who believe in Him eternal life. Through this faith we have eternal life and that is a great treasure, but it doesn't stop there. Otherwise, we would be immediately swept away to heaven.

Instead, we are left here on earth with a new mission – a new identity and a new life. Yet, how many of us simply continue to live as we always had? We may have the same judgements, and prejudices, face the same problems, same worries, same doubts, and chase the same pursuits?

Perhaps we take faith for granted and think it will just grow automatically, but as we know, nothing can flourish without work and nourishment.

When I finally surrendered my life to Christ, God had already been working to connect my wife with some friends at a particular church. He had also led my wife to buy me my first Bible.

I had never owned a Bible, especially one with my name on it. So, one Christmas, before my surrender, my wife gave me an engraved Bible for Christmas.

Many of us like to give that "one big gift" to our loved ones at Christmas. Perhaps it's a television, computer, whatever it may be. This Christmas, my wife's "big gift" to me was this Bible.

Well, my initial reaction was gratitude, but I kept waiting for the "real" gift – the "big" gift, but of course, the Bible was it. So, I was polite. Gave her a kiss and a thank you and put the Bible on a shelf to gather dust.

Months later, as I got off my knees and wiped the tears from my eyes after surrendering my life to Christ, the first thing I went looking for was that Bible. Today, the pages are worn and tattered, and many have fallen from its binding. It's used - well used, but it sits open on my bathroom counter, so that the Word is always before me, and every time I look at it, I am reminded of God's love, who first touched my wife's heart to give me His word.

It was this first Bible I took to our earlier church services. Little did I know at the time, but this church would later prove to be a place God used to create some of the most impactful moments in my life - many already mentioned.

At first, I didn't know the majority of the songs that were being sung, nor did I know where to find many of the verses referenced.

So, being slightly intimidated, we sat as far away from the front of the church as possible – all the way in the back balcony, but in time, we began inching our way forward.

We also joined a small group Bible study class – that was very intimidating, because they would sometimes call on me to pray. I wasn't quite sure what to say, or how to say it, but in time, this too became easier.

This small group eventually led to a smaller group.

A few men decided to get together once a week for an in-depth Bible study. It was the first time I had ever met men passionate about their faith, and who quite honestly had lived pretty wholesome lives.

I recall sharing my testimony with them and watching their mouths seemingly hang open by some of the escapades from my "prior" life.

Yet, through this group of men, my faith began to grow. The "mustard seed" I had, was developing. It was being nurtured through wholesome fellowship, intense Bible study, praise, worship, and prayer.

As time passed, I was eventually asked to take on a leadership role in my small group class, and this eventually led to me teaching the class!

If I had been told I would be teaching an adult Bible study class for nearly 10 years to married couples and would have covered practically every book in the Bible, I would have never believed it.

This is the same guy who was gluttonous, money hungry, selfish, prideful, and pretty much every other "non-Bible teacher" type description one can imagine. Yet, God went to work, as I committed to be a better steward of the faith He had given me.

Please know that all of this is by no means meant to be a preaching session. I'm not a preacher, but I can provide my personal testimony and witness to the overwhelming peace and freedom I have found through my faith, and surrendering my life to Him.

Faith Journey

Many of us worry about tomorrow, next month and next year, but the Bible specifically states not to worry about tomorrow for today has enough problems of its own (Matthew 6:34). I like this statement and appreciate it, because it's good to know God realizes we have problems and that He recognizes that fact. He's basically saying, "Don't stress out, you have enough to deal with now. Focus, and together we'll work through it".

It's comforting to realize, as the saying goes, that I may not know what tomorrow holds, but I do know Who holds tomorrow.

I don't have insight as to where you are on your spiritual journey, but I have been on various levels throughout my life.

I actually attended a Christian elementary school, but later transferred by the fourth grade to the public school system and quickly forgot most of what I learned those earlier years.

However, I believe the foundational spiritual insights I gained earlier in my life never truly left me. For even though I remember when I rarely prayed, or attended church, its seems I eventually came full circle.

It's not that I didn't believe in Jesus as I drifted, it was more like not being aware of my need for Him on a daily basis. I thought I had the will-power and forgot that I needed "His-power" and help.

During college, I couldn't wait to get out and start making money. In the meantime, I was searching for happiness in all the wrong places. Looking back, I realize how lost I was. The academic world enlightens us in so many positive ways, but it also introduces many options and different ways of thinking. As a result, I defined a way of living that suited me, and I justified it as being acceptable and okay.

Thankfully, I eventually came back to the truth, and to the Source of true peace and fulfillment.

Interestingly, I don't regret those "drifter" days,

because they remind me of where I was and that I never want to go back. I did waste some valuable time and if I knew then what I know now, I would have never done the stuff I did, but I'm thankful for the lessons learned. For those hardships help me empathize better, and hopefully allow me to share my testimony in a way others can relate to.

I do remember fearing and worrying about everything though. I feared failing out of college. I feared commitment, I feared falling in love, I feared not being popular enough, I feared not making enough money, and I feared not becoming who I wanted to be. It was later I learned that the spirit of fear does not come from God (Isaiah 41:10).

At the time, I felt everything was dependent upon me, and I was uneasy about being good enough. A benefit of this mindset is that it propelled me to excel in most everything I took on, but the downfall was that I rarely achieved any satisfaction, or reward for my success, because I felt it was only temporary and could be lost any second.

Early in my career, I recall a time when my boss asked me what drove me to be successful at my job – my reply was the fear of failure. Interestingly, I was praised for this and recognized for it. Fear of failure was considered a good a thing – but is it?

To be courageous indicates we overcome our fears, and that is good, but the Bible repeatedly tells us not to fear, but to trust God. Today, I realize trust is a more powerful motivator than fear ever was. It empowers me to give my best regardless of the consequences, because as we know, there are never any guarantees. Therefore, no matter how well we do in our jobs for example, they can always be taken away.

However, when we give our best and trust God with the consequences, we may not like the fact our jobs go away, but we can "trust" there must be a reason. We can leave with our heads high, because we know we gave our best and did all we could. This is where fear as a motivator fails, because it is a performance based approach to life, rather than a faith based one.

You may recall some celebrities and athletes you have seen upon their retirement, or when interviewed about their accomplishments, state that much of their success didn't seem as monumental as they thought it was going to be. In fact, they indicate it was often empty at the top.

I don't want to live like that. I believe we are not created to live with worry, fear, envy, and emptiness, but rather we are to live with confidence, optimism, and gratitude. I also believe that all things work to strengthen and benefit us - even hard times. Quite often, the hard times and struggles are when we tend to learn and grow the most in life and with God. For as many have often said, if we simply obey God, we can trust all the consequences to Him. How nice is that?

THE GIFT OF FAILURE

Failure serving as a gift is definitely true for me. If I hadn't underperformed on the initial entrance exam to enter the University of Georgia's Journalism school, I would never have improved my writing skills and discovered my passion for communication. In addition, if I had never been downsized from an advertising agency, I would have never been forced to learn the financial industry, which is a powerful platform to offer help, hope and encouragement. And if I had never had high cholesterol, I would have never improved my health and lifestyle.

I can go on and on, but you get the point. We grow and improve through our challenges. Even though they seem to be unbearable at the time, we ultimately come out better than before.

I used to wonder about my future and wanted to fast forward my life to see what I would become, but now I don't worry, or at least not as often, because I know no matter what my future holds, it's ultimately good with God in control - and so is yours.

Is maintaining a strong spirituality and faith hard? I think it can be because of distractions. For example, faith can be defined as believing in something we can't see, or at times, can't prove, yet accepting it as truth (Hebrews 11:1). That can be hard, because it doesn't seem natural. After all, we're visual beings, and can get distracted by all the "shiny objects" in this world - yet it is possible. Strengthening one's faith is like exercising, it gets easier with practice and dedication.

Faith, I've learned, is not some powerful force that dwells up inside us. It's simply living one day at a time, trusting God's promises. Doing all the things we do, but living with a peace believing God is who He says He is – taking Him at His word. Trusting that He only wants the best for us, that He's good all the time, protects us, limits our pain, has a purposes for us, has forgiven us, and empowers us to do all things through Him.

Again, this doesn't mean we don't and will not have problems. It doesn't mean we never get sad, or mad. It simply means we live our lives the best we can, seek to know him better, obey Him, and trust what He says. It's believing all things work for an ultimate good, even though we might not see how.

The discovery of what faith is lifted a weight from me. If I acknowledge bad things can happen, but can work towards my ultimate good, my worry diminishes greatly. Clearly, there are consequences to our poor choices, but if we know we can accomplish anything He desires for us, and that He wants the best for us, our fear dwindles. If I believe a part of Him dwells inside me as the Holy Spirit, I am capable of greatness, as He defines it, and can live life to the fullest with courage and confidence.

These beliefs help empower me to improve every aspect of my life. So, with faith none of us can lose. It's an empowered and peaceful way to live. It's our gift and a blessing.

Please note, I still get worried, I still get scared, I still stress out, I still struggle with temptations, and I still fall flat on my face; but I get back up, dust off, and get back in the race. I even get doubtful at times and question things. That's why I make sure I do my best to read Scripture and pray every day, although I'm far from perfect, I'm a lot farther along than I used to be, and my ability to recognize and receive His blessings freely compounds daily.

IS SEEING ALWAYS BELIEVING?

One of the best tools any of us can implement is our perspective and realizing its impact in our life. If we believe something to be true, like God is always good, it literally transforms the way we look at everything that comes our way. Additionally, Henry Ford once said, *"If you think you can do a thing or think you can't do a thing, you're right"*.

This is not simply positive thinking. Although positive thinking can be a good thing, Biblical perspective helps us when a positive mindset falls short.

To illustrate the benefits of a positive outlook, I think of Roger Bannister. Some may know he was the first runner to ever break the four minute mile. Back in the 1950s when he accomplished this feat, no one thought it could be done. In fact, doctors stated the human heart would explode if tried and that he would die, but Bannister was relentless and conditioned his mind to believe it was possible. In his mind he envisioned himself beating four minutes over and over again. Finally, his visions coupled with diligent practice allowed him to accomplish his goal.

Shortly after breaking the four minute mile and the heart explosion myth, other runners stepped out and broke the record too.

You see, no one broke four minutes before, because everyone's mind was conditioned to believe it couldn't be done, but as soon as someone changed that perception, others began to break through. This is the power of the mind, the power of beliefs and the power of commitment.

However, sometimes we may do all Roger did and still come up short – what then? This is when the power of a proper perspective shines through. For if we truly believe in God's promises, goodness, and guidance, we can possess His peace no matter the outcome.

We may experience disappointment, but never have to be without hope. Just imagine the peace and freedom we can possess when we believe God protects us and wants our best - always. This powerful truth was a primary inspiration to my novel, *Highways End*.

For decades I had a quote posted to my bathroom mirror so that I would see it every morning and every night. It says, *"Whatever you vividly imagine, ardently desire, sincerely believe in, enthusiastically act upon and work hard to achieve, must inevitably come to pass"*. I know this isn't necessarily true today, nor should it be. But this is not a bad thing, or me simply being pessimistic.

Rather, if you embrace your deepest desires and goals and singe them on your mind and in your heart and have faith, they still might not be realized - and that's okay. The point is to reach a point of total surrender. To give our hopes and dreams to God and allow Him to transfer His hopes and dreams to us. Then, our dreams and desires are His desires and what a powerful combination that is! To have the desires of God as our inner desires is a true blessing. So, it's not about pursing our dreams, but His.

Years ago, I went through a particular exercise I had heard about, to help me visualize my goals, and recently told my daughter about it. I call it a dream collage, and I gave her a dream journal to keep one going, with the caveat to pray to God about her dreams. I encouraged her to ask Him to plant His dreams into her heart and for her to then write them down.

Here's how it works, simply go through your magazines and cut out every word and picture that reflects your goals and desires. You then create a collage and paste them on a sheet of paper.

This may sound silly, but I did it and still have this potpourri of visual and verbal stimuli taped in my closet. On it, I have everything I wanted to accomplish in my life glaring at me in four-color. I'm forced to visualize my goals, because they're posted right in front of me. I get to track my progress by seeing which goal I've already obtained and am reminded to stay focused by seeing which goals still elude me. At the center of my collage is a dove, representing Christ as my center focus. It's interesting to look at that collage now and how many of those dreams God delivered on, and we're not done yet!

Another way we can track our life adventure with God is by keeping a prayer journal, as mentioned earlier. As we write our prayers down, with the dates we started them, we get to track God's goodness in our life. We even get to see the prayers we are grateful He didn't answer, or allow! Just imagine what a powerful gift this would be to give our children and grandchildren one day.

To continually fuel the pursuit of my goals, my faith is key. However, faith is something that must always be worked on and developed. Just as the body needs water and food, we need to nourish our souls. We eat more than once a week - so should we devote ourselves to feeding our Spirit.

The fact is we have many tools to help us stay focused and disciplined in growing our faith – the Bible being the most important. We must learn not to just read it, but to absorb and seek the lessons to be embedded in our heart. There is no trial, or human desire that is not covered in the Bible. It addresses every human instinct, passion, impulse, and craving, but it also shares how we can overcome any temptation, weakness, and distraction.

If my reading begins to feel routine, I stop and get refocused. I simply sit silently and be still. I wait a moment and then reread the verse and ask for God to open my heart and mind to receive the message I need to prepare me for my day. I also work to remind myself to live for today and not to create worries about tomorrow.

Again, my life belongs to Him. So, it's His job to help guide me in, thru, up, over, around, and/or under challenges that arise - not mine. I am simply the vessel He works through for His purpose. I pray to be courageous enough and wise enough to be open to His will; and thus, strive to do my very best that day in whatever job, or duty is before me.

The only way any of us can gain the strength to improve our finances, enrich our families, maximize our health, and empower our lives is to seek help. We can't do it on our own. No one can – it's too heavy, but through a strong faith, prayerful planning, and a sensitive Spirit, we will gain the support we need to accomplish His goals for us.

Think about it. There is no obstacle, or goal our faith can't penetrate. Being strong and filled-up in our faith impacts our wisdom to be good stewards of money, build a solid family, give and receive genuine love, and enhance our discipline to commit to a healthy lifestyle.

In summary, never forget you may achieve great monetary wealth, but money comes and goes. You may gain the perfect body, but time eventually takes it away, and you may have a strong family, but lack the resources you desire to support them.

In addition, you may have faith, but fail to make it a growth priority. Thus, putting your other stewardship areas and opportunities at risk.

Have you ever seen Christians in financial ruin, completely out of shape, and surrounded by wrecked relationships? Bad things will happen to everyone, and we will make mistakes, but imagine the witness we can be when we allow God to turn these things around for our good, His glory, and to help others in the same areas we stumbled and struggled.

We do not have to be beaten by our circumstances - change is always possible, but like any change, it's never easy.

Am I saying we can have it all? No – but with Christ, we have everything we need. "No good thing will He withhold from those who walk uprightly" (Palm 84:11). God wants the best for all of us! He doesn't want us to live beaten and sorrowful. He wants us to live life abundantly and to positively impact others around us. He wants us to serve as "good shepherds" of the flocks He has entrusted us and to point others to Him.

So, there is no reason we can't be sound money managers, pursue strong family relations, positive health habits, and possess a rock solid faith. It just takes some heavy lifting on our part and baby steps. He will do the rest. If we seek His help, but most importantly, believe in His power and promises. Anything is possible through Christ and to him who believes (Mark 9:23).

Envision what you desire out of life in prayer – does it reach beyond merely yourself? Then, make it real in your mind and pursue it in faith. For without the primary success and goal being our Lord – all other successes are meaningless and empty.

After all, cars eventually rust and homes and money can burn. However, our faith is everlasting. These are many of the "worthless things" that can distract us from the "Primary" thing.

FROM SAVED TO SURRENDERED

I want to share one last climatic moment in my life. As stated earlier, surrendering my life to Christ was the biggest, but then came one of the greatest testing moments I could have ever imagined.

It came during a transition in my job. I had been earning a very good income and an opportunity came my way to make even more. However, it required me to move my family. I know that doesn't sound like a big deal. People do it all the time. Yet, we really didn't want to move, or feel God's calling to.

We get to raise our kids in the house I grew up in. We have friends and family all around us and are very involved in our church and community. So, moving just wasn't something we were all that excited about – but the money being offered was very attractive and hard to resist. However, as I stated, my life was now surrendered to Christ, and even though I admittedly enjoy making money, I never want money to lead my life. I desire to live for Christ. That means, He must lead me and my decisions, not money.

So, as divine intervention would have it, another

offer was presented to me as well, but it wasn't paying nearly what the other position did, or could. However, the introduction to this new position actually came through my church, with little to no involvement on my part at all. The larger income position came through a direct connection I had made.

But the layers add on. The position offering less allowed our family to stay in our community and continue a passion I have in life – teaching financial stewardship and building teams.

It was down to decision time. Do I move my family, which no one wanted, or felt led to do, and take the significant pay increase, or take the lower paying job, less than I had made in a decade and allow my family to stay where they all wanted to stay? Again, the pay was good, but just not what I had been making, or could be making.

So, I prayed and I didn't like what I was hearing. God was speaking to me in various ways to take the lower paying job and keep my family in our home. I just couldn't understand why. Why not move, why not take the more money, save it and then just move back? But that's not what I was feeling led to do.

My wife and I hadn't shared with our kids the two specific options we had. Rather, we were simply praying as a family for the "right" job. Then one night during family prayers, my daughter spoke out loud what was in her heart, adding to the confirmation I was already feeling in mine. She prayed for God to help Daddy accept a job that allowed us to stay in our home and not move. Again, she had no idea we even had an option to move, or to stay.

The confirmation of what to do was building up. I then told my wife later on what I knew we had to do. She thought that meant to move, because obviously, her driven, corporate climbing husband would never settle for less money than he had been making, or could make. Surely, I wouldn't pass up something so enticing as moving to the coast and making more!

The good news is, even though she didn't want to move, she was willing. She was willing to do whatever God led us to do, and so was I. We were all willing to move, if God wanted it. I didn't tell her my decision was to stay. I wanted one more night of prayer - to argue and debate with God one last time.

That night while I was in prayer, I was completely nauseous and sick to my stomach. It was like something was being pulled out of me. It was a time of complete surrender. I felt like I was going to get sick right there on the floor. For I knew God wanted me to pass on the higher paying job and take the lesser paying one. Again, it wasn't a matter of the work and responsibilities of the jobs - both offered work I enjoyed and excited about. This was all about money - something that had a hold of me for a long time. For my whole life I just wanted to have overflowing riches.

Maybe because I remember having very little growing up. Maybe because I remember thinking more money could solve more problems - and like I mentioned earlier, maybe I believed the lie that my self-worth was defined by my net-worth. Also, maybe I looked to "treasure" as my source of security more than I trusted God?

All of this was being surrendered that night. Instead of going for the money, I chose what I felt God was leading me to do.

Was it easy? Absolutely not, but it was a true blessing. My family rejoiced knowing we got to stay home, and they love the place I went to work. For it is a great company with great people. Did I miss the money? Of course, but not more than missing out on what God wants for me.

For in the end, I don't believe God cares about the money. He wants my surrender and my obedience. And I believe He was testing and refining my commitment to live a surrendered life to Him, and He knew money was a huge driver for me. I believe it was an Abraham moment. Just like when God told Abraham to sacrifice his son, He knew what Abraham was going to do, but it was an opportunity for Abraham to sharpen his resolve. Sharpen his commitment. Sharpen his faith.

That's what happened to me. I'm not against moving, or taking more money. My point in sharing this part of my ever growing testimony is simply this – trust God and follow Him, not the money, or whatever that "thing" is that competes for prioritized position in your life outside of God.

In summary, our faith cannot remain lukewarm and something we take for granted. It is a gift we are to steward. That means it requires commitment and investment, and we do this with intentionality.

Therefore, let us not neglect all the ways to

strengthen our faith - such as committed fellowship with a body of believers on a weekly basis. Church shouldn't be a have-to-do for us, but rather a want-to-do. For it is where we learn, grow, and get to encourage others in their Christian walk.

Let us also commit to daily prayer and Bible study. This is an essential – again, not as a have-to-do, but a want-to-do part of our lifestyle. Spending time with our Creator, our Lord, our King, our Savior – this time is invaluable to our lives. For He knows us best, wants our best, and can direct us to His best - but this requires we give Him our best. He will then take care of orchestrating all the providential details.

V

RAGS TO RICHES

"The price of anything is the amount of life you exchange for it".[12]

- Henry David Thoreau

Have you already started your heavy lifting? I hope so. For the perfectionists out there, we must realize we will never completely perfect every area we have highlighted. It's impossible because that would be perfection and no one is perfect, or can be. We all fall short.

However, our goal is to actively, not passively, pursue improvement in each stewardship area and to identify our weaknesses and strengths. Knowing our areas of strength allows us to improve our weaker ones and close in on our true potential.

Even though we may never achieve full capacity, we can always reach higher. A cross-country coach for my daughter once made a great illustration to this point. She asked everyone to raise their hand as high as they could. She then asked everyone to reach higher – the interesting thing was everyone could reach even higher.

The point is, we may think we have reached and given all we can, but typically there is always more we can give – and always higher we can go.

We want to stretch ourselves while having fun engaging our purpose in life. It should be stimulating realizing our growth in each stewardship area, and it's important to recognize it.

With each new challenge, or step we take in furthering our goals, our acknowledgement is healthy. Recognizing our achievements and making improvements is also giving God praise.

He desires us to leave enriching legacies and to be good stewards, good disciples, and good disciple-makers. The key is not giving ourselves all the credit – for as we know, He is the foundation. What we have are gifts from Him, and we celebrate what we have been given. I am grateful for His help in making me a better steward of all He has entrusted to my care.

I have no doubt you will get to where God wants you to go and that you will be blessed in it, if you trust Him in all your ways. I honestly hope our lives cross paths one day. In a way, they already have, but I'd love to meet you in person and hear how you're doing on your redefined "wealth" journey.

My prayer is that you gained some valuable insights you can use from a person who nearly lost it all due to selfish ambition. My hope is to share my faith, and pass along lessons I have learned along the way to benefit others and bring glory to God.

In summary, we looked at strategies to maximize our financial stewardship, including how to use debt wisely, avoid costly mistakes, and secure a sound financial future. We discussed how to help prioritize and support a strong and loving legacy within our families. We also shared some processes to help nurture good health, including our physical and mental vitality. We then completed our "redefining wealth" initiative by developing, and hopefully strengthening, our belief system and faith. The realization that we can do all things, through Christ, gives us hope and reassurance that our dreams are viable and worthy of pursuit.

Even if we never make millions, our lives can still be "rich" in faith, healthy habits, strong stewardship, and loving relationships. For as we now know, wealth is not measured solely by material goods. True wealth is pursuing levels of peace in our primary gifts of faith, family, fitness, and finance. Money alone is not a substitute for these things and never can be. Rather, it can be a source of loneliness and loss without Christ.

Money is simply a tool we must be educated on in order to live fiscally responsible lives. Otherwise, we can become slaves to debt and material goods.

Money is not the first step in achieving success. Instead, it all begins with our perspective of money, our prioritization of it, and then our preparations to be good stewards of it. We cannot effectively accomplish this without our faith in Jesus Christ and realizing there is more to life than material gain. We have been given much – money is ultimately the "cheapest" thing we have. For without a growing faith, nourished family, and positive health habits, what do we truly have?

My struggle with wanting more possessions, positions, promotions , and praise hasn't ended, but thankfully my blinders have been removed. I have to take up my "cross" daily in many ways and pray for God to keep my eyes off worthless things. To keep my life true to Him.

Ultimately, we have all been given *time, talents, treasures,* and *testimonies* to distribute. These have been entrusted to us all, but how they get spent varies greatly.

Faith guides and directs us on how to invest them wisely. I used to squander my time, talent, treasures, and testimony greatly, or spend them solely to benefit myself, but I now pray to use them mightily in the areas of my faith, family, fitness, and finances.

We only have a limited time to make impact in this world. As the Bible reminds us in Ephesians 5:16 – "let us therefore make the most of every opportunity."

One last insight I'd like to share is a quote by Norman Vincent Peale revealing his opinion to the secret of life. He said, *"The secret of life isn't in what happens to you, but what you do with what happens to you"*.

Let's always choose, as the saying goes, to make lemonade out of lemons, and to never settle for discouragement. Let's make our time here what God desires it to be -opportunities to serve, bless, share, and enjoy life as an adventure with and trusting in Him.

My prayer is that we begin immediately. Changing our poor beliefs and habits to positive ones can be done successfully, but it takes commitment to make it happen.

Now, it's time to take action, if you haven't already. Write down specific goals for each stewardship area you will complete and set a deadline. Make yourself commit and list 7 reasons why you want each goal. Make challenging goals and provide the steps you will take to achieve them in prayer.

Strive for true success realizing it is not measured materially, but through more enduring accomplishments such as impacting lives for the better, giving of one's self and living as a testimony to what's possible through faith.

Lastly, look at your goal list and consider its overall direction. Is it to promote yourself? Or, is it to promote a higher calling of purpose? Goals that promote self usually end up feeling hollow, if we accomplish them at all. However, we tap into powerful resources when we reach beyond self and towards God – that's where our purpose and endless blessings abound! For we are not to hoard, but to share.

Please note there's nothing wrong with being materially rich. We can do a lot of good with money! Again, money is not the root of evil - its people that get greedy and corrupt. Even the wealthy and wise king Solomon once said, "The blessing of the Lord brings wealth, and he adds no trouble to it," (Proverbs 10:22). Our expanded definition and perspective of wealth however brings this verse into greater illumination!

Also, there's nothing wrong with pursuing good health and looking our best. There's nothing wrong with pursuing strong, nurturing relationships; and there's nothing wrong with pursuing a bold faith in Jesus Christ.

Faith Walk

When my novel, *Highways End* was released, an article was written describing how it was a Christian novel inspired by Ecclesiastes, my faith, and my own vain attempts to find satisfaction "under the sun". This same article was also distributed and shared on various social media outlets, and parts of my testimony were on display like never before.

My emotional reaction to the response this article received was a mixture of exhilaration and vulnerability.

One of the whispers of insecurity that ran through my mind was how I would forever be labeled as a "nice guy" - and we all know how the nice guys finish don't we? Last! Or, at least that's how the saying goes.

Shameful to admit, but it's true – I worried about how others were going to perceive me, especially in the corporate world. For a nice guy can never effectively run a business, because they're too nice; and being too nice means you can't make the hard decisions. In addition, nice folks are easily taken advantage of and manipulated – right? All of these clichés and falsehoods ran through my mind.

I was temporarily distracted by the thoughts of self-preservation, and the potential professional collateral damage for taking such a bold position as a Christian for all to see, hear, and read. Sad, isn't it?

Suddenly, God broke through this cloud of deception and spoke truth to my heart. He reminded me of my earlier prayers. He reminded me that years ago, and to this day, I ask Him to use my life, including my time, talents, treasures, testimonies, books and blog as platforms to share the gospel, my faith, and bring glory to Him. But most importantly, He reminded me to His Son's precious words and promise in Matthew 10:32, where He declares that whoever acknowledges Him before others, He will also acknowledge them before God. He reminded me that I am to obey Him, courageously share Him in love, serve Him, and to ultimately trust Him with all the consequences.

As a result, His peace filled my heart, and I prayed for His forgiveness for thinking such thoughts .

As a side, we may not always be able to control the thoughts that flood our mind, but we can choose whether we allow them to linger. Instead, we can recognize them for the rubbish they are, and flush them away.

Once again, God lifted my head, restored my perspective, and refreshed my purpose with His overwhelming love.

May we never forget our life is more than our work, money, or anything else that may distract us from our primary directive. Rather, as good stewards, our faith, family, fitness, and finances can serve as outlets to offer hope and encouragement to others. This frees us from the "workaholic" mindset, because life no longer centers around us, but God.

However, I recognize not all have received God's free gift of salvation, or surrendered their lives fully to Christ. Thankfully, this too can change with the greatest decision any of us will ever make - and when it does, He changes everything.

Therefore, I pray we go for it - and pursue a courageous life of faith that will take us from selfish rags to true stewardship riches!

NOTES

Dagan J. Sharpe

AUTHOR BIO

With over seventeen years of experience in the financial industry, Dagan has various financial licenses and experience in investments, insurance, trust, banking and lending. He has served in both community banks and as a national director for one of the largest financial services firms in America.

As a communications major from the University of Georgia's Grady College of Journalism, Dagan's passion is using his broad and varied background to provide encouragement to other believers in their walk with Christ - and to further the gospel through his service as a deacon in his church, an adult Bible study teacher, and through his various books, and international blog, *CareerCall.org*

Dagan and his wife, Jennifer, live in Augusta, Georgia with their two children and love anything that has to do with the water. They also enjoy an active lifestyle of fellowship among their loving friends and family.

Dagan J. Sharpe

FULL DISCLOSURE

ENDNOTES

1. https://www.goodreads.com/quotes/1310335-a-time-comes-when-you-need-to-stop-waiting-for

2. https://en.oxforddictionaries.com/definition/wealth

3. http://www.goodreads.com/quotes/321104-inch-by-inch-life-s-a-cinch-yard-by-yard-life-s

4. http://www.azquotes.com/quote/961860

5. https://en.wikipedia.org/wiki/Wall_Street_Journal_prime_rate

6. http://www.investopedia.com/ask/answers/042415/what-average-annual-return-sp-500.asp

7. https://www.google.com/amp/s/www.fool.com/amp/investing/general/2014/09/28/25-best-warren-buffett-quotes.aspx

8. http://www.anewdayanewme.com/dr-fuhrman-immunity-solution-g-bombs-superfoods-that-can-heal-and-prevent-disease/

9. https://www.goodreads.com/quotes/62266-what-can-you-do-to-promote-world-peace-go-home

10. https://www.goodreads.com/quotes/237998-the-first-wealth-is-health

11. https://www.goodreads.com/quotes/16312-faith-is-taking-the-first-step-even-when-you-can-t

12. https://www.goodreads.com/quotes/103804-the-cost-of-a-thing-is-the-amount-of-what

Dagan J. Sharpe